A FIELD GUIDE T~
MAM

Cath Jones and Steve Parish

Steve Parish ™
P U B L I S H I N G

Introduction...7
  A History of Australian Mammals.....................................8
  Classifying and Naming Mammals...............................10
  Habitats of Australian Mammals.....................................14
  Some Australian Habitat Types.....................................16
Monotremes..19
  Platypus..20
  Short-beaked Echidna...24
Marsupials...29
  Carnivorous Marsupials..30
    Quolls...31
    Tasmanian Devil...36
    Small Dasyurids...40
    Numbat..48
  Marsupial Moles 52
  Bandicoots and the Bilby.......................................54
  Herbivorous Marsupials 63
    Koala..64
    Wombats 70
    Possums..76
      Pygmy-possums..82
      Wrist-winged gliders, Striped Possum and Leadbeater's Possum....86
      The Greater Glider and Ringtail Possums.......................90
      Brushtail Possums, Cuscuses and the Scaly-tailed Possum.........96
      Honey Possum..100
      Feathertail Glider 102
    Macropods..105
      Potoroos, Bettongs and Rat-kangaroo...........................114
      Hare-wallabies..118
      Pademelons...120
      Quokka..122
      Swamp Wallaby...123
      Tree-kangaroos 124
      Rock-wallabies..126
      Nailtail Wallabies 134
      Kangaroos, Wallaroos and Typical Wallabies 136
Placentals 147
    Bats..148
      Megabats 149
      Microbats 150
    Rodents 158
    Dingo 166
    Seals 170
    Dugong..176
    Whales and Dolphins..178
    Introduced Mammals...193
Mammals and People 198
  Watching Wildlife..198
  Photographing Wildlife...200
  Wildlife Conservation 206
  Australia's National Parks Map.....................................208
References and Further Information 210
Glossary..211
Index of Common Names...212
Index of Scientific Names 214
Abbreviations and Symbols...215

INTRODUCTION

Australia, the world's smallest and second driest continent, is, in its wide range of habitats, home to a remarkable variety of mammals. Some are so well known they have become national symbols. Others are seldom seen and do not even have common names.

Australia's native mammals have evolved in isolation over millions of years and many are found nowhere else in the world. Each one has a body and lifestyle suited to the realities of living in a sometimes harsh and unforgiving land.

Their continued survival depends on our willingness to ensure that habitats are maintained and on their ability to adapt to changing environmental conditions and to cope with introduced fauna.

This book guides readers through the main groups of native mammals as it reveals their hidden lives and fascinating survival strategies. Tips on where and how to look for these creatures and more than 150 individual profiles provide a handy reference for wildlife watchers at home and in the wild.

Ian Morris

Above: Common Ringtail Possum.
Opposite: Female Koala and back-riding joey.

Australia's unique mammals, such as this Red Kangaroo, evolved over millions of years.

A History of Australian Mammals

Modern technology and old-fashioned deduction have helped piece together the evolutionary history of Australia's native mammals, a fascinating but incomplete saga, incomplete because it is clear that, while there is more evidence to be uncovered, much has been obliterated. It is a global story that links past and present by comparing the body structures and chemistry of living mammals with the fossilised remains of extinct mammals.

Fossil evidence suggests that mammals had evolved from reptilian ancestors while Australia was still part of a giant southern landmass called Gondwana. When tectonic forces cast Australia adrift from Antarctica between 45 and 38 million years ago, its mammalian cargo included monotremes and marsupials. Placental representatives were limited to bats and a primitive type of baleen whale.

As continental drift carried Australia northwards, its climate, landforms and vegetation changed many times. Alternating ice ages and greenhouse ages saw sea levels rise and fall while forests and wetlands expanded and contracted. The mammals that were adaptable enough to exploit the new habitats and food sources created by changing environmental conditions diversified and proliferated.

✘ Among the many fossils found in Mammoth Cave in WA were the bones of *Zaglossus hacketti*, a sheep-sized echidna.

✘ An opalised lower jawbone about 120 million years old found at Lightning Ridge, New South Wales, is the world's oldest known monotreme fossil.

✘ Riversleigh in Queensland and the Lake Eyre Basin in South Australia have rich marsupial fossil records that date back as far as 55 million years.

✘ Fossilised dolphin-like bones and teeth up to 23 million years old have been found in south-east Victoria and near Lake Frome in South Australia.

A model of an injured *Propleopus* (a carnivorous predecessor of today's kangaroo) is part of a display at the Riversleigh Fossils Centre at Mount Isa, Queensland.

About 15 million years ago Australia began drying out. Grasslands and woodlands became the dominant types of vegetation. These increasingly arid conditions favoured animals that were water and energy efficient and could breed quickly after sporadic rain.

By 5 million years ago placental mammals, such as baleen whales, sperm whales, dolphins and seals, cruised the oceans covering Australia's continental shelf. Marsupial mammals continued to dominate Australia's terrestrial habitats despite an influx of rodents and bats from south-east Asia as the gap between the two continents narrowed. When humans crossed that gap more than 60,000 years ago, the reign of the megafauna was coming to an end and, for the first time, Australian marsupials and monotremes faced the challenge of coexisting with large placental mammals.

The influx of European humans and their entourages of exotic animals since the 1700s, has triggered an unprecedented rate of environmental change and an alarming decline in the number and variety of native mammals.

Some scientists predict that the combined effects of human activities and the current cycle of global warming now threaten the long-term survival of Australia's remaining native mammals.

Megafauna

The rise of giant species of marsupials during the Pleistocene epoch has been linked to the gradual spread of woodland and grassland habitats. The largest of the marsupial megafauna was *Diprotodon*, a herbivorous, rhinoceros-sized relative of today's wombats. Others included *Procoptodon*, a leaf-eating kangaroo 2.5 m high and weighing 270 kg; and the flesh-eating marsupial lion, *Thylacoleo*, that weighed about 150 kg and had partly opposable thumbs on its front paws. Climate change and human activity are thought to have contributed to the demise of the megafauna.

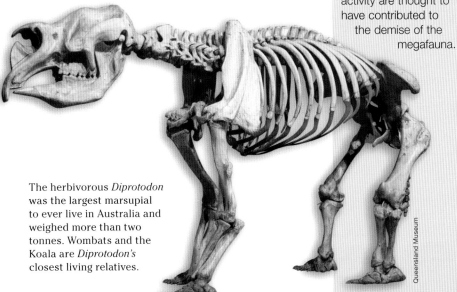

The herbivorous *Diprotodon* was the largest marsupial to ever live in Australia and weighed more than two tonnes. Wombats and the Koala are *Diprotodon's* closest living relatives.

Queensland Museum

Classifying and Naming Mammals

All living things are described according to a system of taxonomy devised in the 18th century. The classification into a hierarchical system of groups helps scientists describe and identify them and determine their evolutionary relationships. Classification levels go from general to specific and each level describes the characteristic features of a group of organisms. Animals' diagnostic features are based on body structures, DNA, blood proteins and functional processes.

A mammal's **scientific name** is used worldwide and does not change unless it is reclassified. It consists of two or three latinised words and is written in reverse order to English names. The first, or genus, name describes the group of similar animals to which it belongs. The second, or species, name usually describes a distinctive feature of that specific mammal. A third, or subspecies, name is used to distinguish a race or subpopulation within a species. For example, *Macropus robustus* is the scientific name of the Common Wallaroo, and it means "robust long-foot".

A mammal's **common name** can vary from place to place: *Macropus robustus* is also known as the Euro, Hill Kangaroo, Eastern Grey Wallaroo, Red Wallaroo and Biggada.

The Common Wallaroo *Macropus robustus* is classified as follows:

Kingdom	**Animalia**	multi-celled organism that is not a plant, bacterium or fungus
Phylum	**Chordata**	animal with nerve chord along back
Subphylum	**Vertebrata**	chordate with jointed backbones
Class	**Mammalia**	vertebrate with mammary glands
Subclass	**Marsupialia**	mammal whose young are born partially developed and may be protected by a pouch
Order	**Diprotodontia**	marsupial with one pair of lower incisors
Family	**Macropodidae**	diprotodont with long hind feet
Genus	**Macropus**	macropod with typical features
Species	***robustus***	robust

Class: Mammalia

All mammals belong to the class **Mammalia** and are classified into three subclasses according to the way they reproduce. The following gives the taxonomic breakdown to family; some families are further divided into subfamilies.

Eastern Quoll family

Monotremes – Prototherian Mammals

Female monotremes lay soft-shelled eggs. The baby hatches after a brief incubation, blind, furless and with hind legs incompletely formed. It feeds on milk that oozes from mammary ducts on its mother's belly. An echidna carries her eggs and developing young in a pouch, while a Platypus incubates her eggs and nurses her young in a nesting burrow.

Subclass: Prototheria

Order: Monotremata
Family: Ornithorhynchidae (Platypus)
Family: Tachyglossidae (Short-beaked Echidna)

Marsupials – Metatherian Mammals

Female marsupial mammals bear partially developed young after a brief gestation period. A newborn marsupial is blind, furless and its tail and hindlimbs are incomplete. Using its strong forelimbs, the tiny baby drags itself from the cloaca and continues development attached to a teat on its mother's belly which may be protected by a pouch or temporary folds of skin.

Short-beaked Echidna

Subclass: Marsupialia (Metatheria)

Order: Dasyuromorphia
Superfamily: Dasyuroidea
Family: Dasyuridae (quolls, dibblers, pseudantechinuses, parantechinuses, Kowari, Mulgara, Ampurta, Kaluta, Tasmanian Devil, phascogales, antechinuses, planigales, ningauis, dunnarts, Kultarr)
Family: Myrmecobiidae (Numbat)
Family: Thylacinidae (Thylacine)

Order: Peramelemorphia
Superfamily: Perameloidea
Family: Peramelidae (bandicoots, bilbies)
Family: Peroryctidae (Rufous Spiny Bandicoot)

Yellow-footed Antechinus

Koala

Order: Diprotodontia
Suborder: Vombatiformes
Family: Phascolarctidae (Koala)
Family: Vombatidae (wombats)
Suborder: Phalangerida
Superfamily: Burramyoidea
Family: Burramyidae (pygmy-possums)
Superfamily: Petauroidea
Family: Petauridae (Striped Possum, Leadbeater's Possum, wrist-winged gliders)
Family: Pseudocheiridae (ringtail possums, Greater Glider)
Superfamily: Tarsipedoidea
Family: Tarsipedidae (Honey Possum)
Family: Acrobatidae (Feathertail Glider)
Superfamily: Phalangeroidea
Family: Phalangeridae (brushtail possums, cuscuses, Scaly-tailed Possum)
Superfamily: Macropodoidea
Family: Hypsiprymnodontidae (Musky Rat-kangaroo)
Family: Potoroidae (potoroos, bettongs)
Family: Macropodidae (tree-kangaroos, hare-wallabies, wallabies, wallaroos, kangaroos, nailtail wallabies, rock-wallabies, pademelons, Quokka, Swamp Wallaby)

Order: Notoryctemorphia
Family: Notoryctidae (marsupial moles)

Red-legged Pademelon

Placentals – Eutherian Mammals

Subclass: Eutheria

Placental, or Eutherian, mammals give birth to fully formed young that develop inside the mother's body with the aid of a placenta. This mass of tissue allows nutrients and wastes to pass between the mother and foetus, and is expelled following birth (the afterbirth). Newborns are sparsely covered with hair, and eyes and limbs are well developed. Young suckle milk from the female's teats until they reach independence.

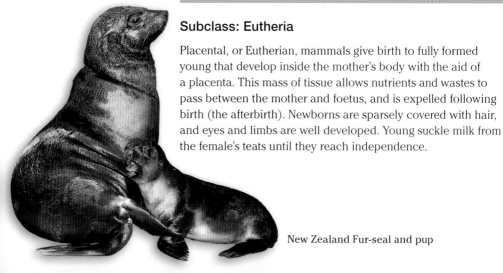

New Zealand Fur-seal and pup

Order: Chiroptera
Suborder: Megachiroptera (megabats)
Family: Pteropodidae (blossom-bats, tube-nosed bats, fruit-bats, flying-foxes)

Suborder: Microchiroptera (microbats)
Family: Megadermatidae (Ghost Bat)
Family: Rhinolophidae (horseshoe-bats)
Family: Hipposideridae (leafnosed-bats)
Family: Emballonuridae (sheathtail-bats)
Family: Molossidae (freetail-bats)
Family: Vespertilionidae (Golden-tipped Bat, bentwing-bats, Tube-nosed Insectivorous Bat, long-eared bats, "typical" bats)

Order: Rodentia
Family: Muridae (rats, mice, melomys)

Grey-headed Flying-fox

Order: Sirenia
Family: Dugongidae (Dugong)

Order: Cetacea
Suborder: Mysticeti (baleen whales)
Family: Balaenidae (Southern Right Whale)
Family: Balaenopteridae (minke, Sei, Bryde's, Blue, Fin, Humpback Whales)
Family: Neobalaenidae (Pygmy Right Whale)

Suborder: Odontoceti (toothed whales)
Family: Delphinidae (dolphins, killer whales, pilot whales, Melon-headed Whale)
Family: Phocoenidae (Spectacled Porpoise)
Family: Physeteridae (sperm whales)
Family: Ziphiidae (beaked whales)

Greater Stick-nest Rat

Order: Carnivora
Family: Otariidae (sea-lions, fur-seals)
Family: Phocidae (earless seals)
Family: Canidae (Dingo, Red Fox)
Family: Felidae (Feral Cat)

Order: Lagomorpha
Family: Leporidae (Rabbit, Hare)

Order: Perissodactyla
Family: Equidae (Brumby, Donkey)

Order: Artiodactyla
Family: Suidae (Feral Pig)
Family: Camelidae (One-humped Camel)
Family: Bovidae (cattle, Swamp Buffalo, Feral Goat)
Family: Cervidae (deer)

Dingo

Habitats of Australian Mammals

Australia may be the world's smallest continent, but it is a land of contrasting natural environments that provide a diversity of habitats for mammals.

A habitat is a physical location usually described in terms of its climate, landforms and vegetation. It is the place where an animal can find the food, shelter, mates and breeding sites it needs to survive as an individual and as a species. An ideal habitat also has a limited number of the animal's competitors and predators.

Some animals have specialised needs that can only be met by conditions in a particular location. Others can be quite at home in several habitats. They may feed in one and shelter in another, or move between habitats on a seasonal basis.

Australian Climatic Regions

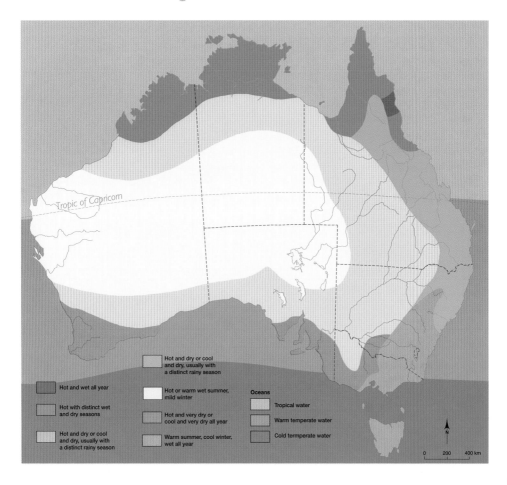

Tropic of Capricorn

Hot and dry or cool and dry, usually with a distinct rainy season

Hot and wet all year

Hot or warm wet summer, mild winter

Oceans

Hot with distinct wet and dry seasons

Tropical water

Hot and very dry or cool and very dry all year

Warm temperate water

Hot and dry or cool and dry, usually with a distinct rainy season

Warm summer, cool winter, wet all year

Cold termperate water

0   200   400 km

Australia and its coastal seas provide a surprising diversity of habitats for marine and terrestrial mammals. Between the sharply contrasting physical forms and climatic conditions of desert and forest, mountaintop and seafloor, are the subtle variations in environmental conditions that create so many different places to live. However, the challenge of surviving in a land characterised by flood and drought, extreme temperatures and bushfires tests even the hardiest of species.

Native vegetation is a signal element in mammal habitats. Having evolved together over such a long time, many species of plants and mammals enjoy mutually beneficial relationships. In some cases, one cannot survive without the other. Habitat loss or degradation, whether occuring naturally or through human activity, is a major factor in the extinction of native mammals.

Australian Vegetation

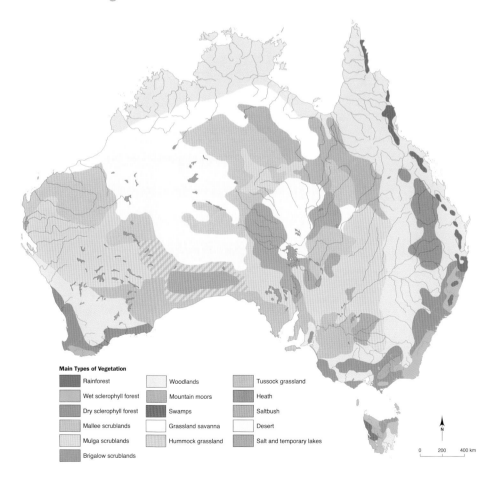

Main Types of Vegetation

Rainforest	Woodlands	Tussock grassland	
Wet sclerophyll forest	Mountain moors	Heath	
Dry sclerophyll forest	Swamps	Saltbush	
Mallee scrublands	Grassland savanna	Desert	
Mulga scrublands	Hummock grassland	Salt and temporary lakes	
Brigalow scrublands			

0   200   400 km

Some Australian Habitat Types

Rainforest

Forest

Woodlands

Shrublands

Grasslands

Wetland

Ocean

Altered Landscape

MONOTREMES

Egg-laying mammals have been around in some form since dinosaurs ruled the Earth. Fossil evidence suggests monotremes originated in the land mass that became Australia and spread northwards before the final break-up of Gondwana. They have never been as diverse or numerous as marsupial and placental mammals, and there are now only three species of monotremes in the world.

The word monotreme means *one hole* and refers to the single opening by which urine, faeces and eggs leave the body. This feature, with egg laying and the arrangement of the shoulder and collar bones, is a legacy of their reptilian ancestry.

Unlike other mammals, monotremes do not have whiskers or teats. Their less sophisticated, smaller brains may have disadvantaged them in terms of adaptability, but, like marsupials, their slightly lower body temperature and metabolic rate make them a little more energy efficient.

The amphibious Platypus (left) and ant- and termite-eating Short-beaked Echidna (above) survive in Australia by exploiting resources few other mammals use.

Platypus
Ornithorhynchus anatinus

✗ Fat stored in the tail can be used for energy when food is limited.

✗ If not moving, a Platypus can remain underwater for up to 11 minutes but normally for only 1–2 minutes while foraging.

✗ Aborigines and European settlers hunted the Platypus for its lustrous fur.

✗ Males have a 15 mm long venomous spur on the outside ankle of each hind foot. Females shed their rudimentary spurs when young.

✗ A Platypus may utter a low growl when disturbed.

✗ Picking up a male Platypus can result in a jab from its spur. This can cause muscular weakness and a rash but is not life-threatening.

Platypus

The first time European scientists saw a preserved specimen of a Platypus in 1798, they thought it was a cleverly crafted fake. The Platypus again confounded scientists when they discovered it had mammary glands but was also found to lay eggs. But this improbable animal was neither a hoax nor an evolutionary link between reptiles and placental mammals.

Although the Platypus is the only living member of the **Ornithorhynchidae** family, recent fossil finds indicate several different species of platypuses have existed during the past 120 million years. Its unique body and aquatic lifestyle have made the present-day Platypus a winner in the survival stakes.

The amphibious Platypus has webbed feet and a sleek, waterproof coat.

Webbing on the front feet extends and fans out to form paddles.

Fit for Survival

This remarkable animal spends up to 12 hours a day in the water, mostly between dusk and dawn. Its smooth swimming style is powered by alternate strokes of the front legs and over-sized webbing on the front feet. Its broad tail acts as a rudder and its hind feet are used to steer and brake.

When it dives to hunt underwater, the Platypus closes its eyes, ears and nostrils. It detects prey by waving its sensitive bill from side to side about two or three times a second. Worms, shrimps, insect larvae and other small animals are collected from the bottom or snapped up in passing and stored in cheek pouches.

The Platypus then returns to the surface where it floats, spread-eagled, as it grinds up its food between the horny ridges that replace the milk teeth in adults.

The Platypus is meticulous about grooming its fur. Its thick coat has an inner layer of fine hairs that traps air to insulate the body. The outer layer of long, flat hairs, that streamlines the body and repels water, moults continually. Grooming keeps the coat in good order and condition.

A Sixth Sense

A Platypus's rubbery bill is covered with thousands of tiny pores. Some pores have nerves that are sensitive to touch; others detect electrical fields generated by moving prey. This kind of sensory information probably gives an image of underwater hunting grounds.

Peter Marsack, Lochman Transparencies

On land, the Platypus folds back the extendible webbing on its front feet.

A Platypus at the entrance to its burrow.

Dave Watts, ANT Photo Library

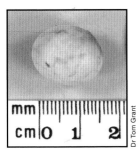

Dr Tom Grant

The egg has a rubbery texture.

✘ A Platypus egg is 17 mm long and has a sticky coating.

✘ A Platypus hatchling is about 15 mm long.

✘ There are more than 600 hairs per mm² in Platypus fur.

✘ Females supplying milk to larger nestlings can consume their body weight in food each day.

✘ Adult males become more aggressive and their venom glands enlarge during the mating season.

A Web-footed Burrower

When it is not foraging, grooming or sleeping, the Platypus rests in a burrow above the water level. The burrow has one or two dome-shaped entrances, usually concealed by tree roots. When walking or digging, the Platypus folds the web extensions back over the soles of its front feet and supports itself on its knuckles. While a Platypus moves quite quickly on land, it is no match for a Red Fox or dog and some are killed by these predators, especially during droughts when Platypuses must move between pools.

Laying Eggs

During the breeding season, pairs engage in an elaborate aquatic courtship lasting several days. After mating takes place in the water, the male resumes his solitary habits while the female digs a complex burrow, up to 30 metres long, about half a metre above the water's surface. The snug egg chamber is lined with damp vegetation and the tunnel is sealed with plugs of mud ready to block off floodwater and predators.

She lays one to three eggs and curls up to incubate them between her tail and belly. The eggs hatch in about 10–12 days. The mother warms and suckles her young for the first few days. When she leaves the nest to hunt, she bundles the babies into a protective cocoon of vegetation. The young are two-thirds adult size by the time they are weaned and independent at age four to five months.

Captive breeding

Captive Platypuses appear to be reluctant breeders, with only four documented successes during the past 60 years. The first captive-bred Platypus was hatched in a tank enclosure at Healesville Sanctuary, Victoria, in 1943. Twin males followed in 1999 and a single male in 2001. In 2003, twin females hatched in a recreated habitat at Taronga Zoo, New South Wales.

A carer and Platypus at Healesville Sanctuary.

Finding Platypuses

Dawn and dusk or overcast winter days are the best times to look for Platypuses. Find a spot on a high bank overlooking a freshwater creek, lake or dam. Scan the surface, preferably with binoculars, for its distinctive V-shaped wake. Check beside the water for tracks and small, irregular shaped scats.

Location Tips

→ Eungella NP, Qld
→ Upper Murray River, Vic
→ Kangaroo and Wingecarribee Rivers, NSW
→ Lake Dobson, Mt Field NP, Tas

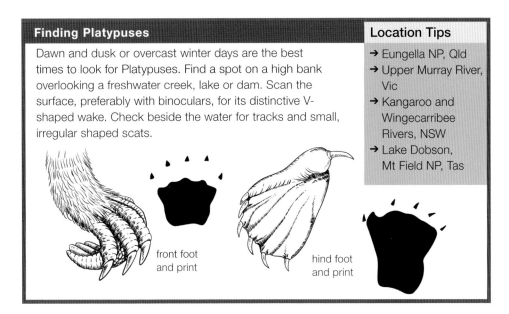

front foot and print

hind foot and print

Platypus *Ornithorhynchus anatinus* (duck-like bird snout)

The world's only species of Platypus is found in eastern Australia from Cooktown to Tasmania and along the Murray River system through Victoria to the South Australian border.

Habitat: Tropical rainforest to alpine heath with permanent, freshwater lakes, dams, creeks or rivers. **Behaviour:** Amphibious, solitary, mostly nocturnal. **Diet:** Predominantly freshwater invertebrates, and occasionally small fish and frogs. **Breeding:** August through October depending on latitude; females can be mature at 2 years. **Lifespan:** Up to 21 years. **Features:** Thick, soft fur is waterproof, dark brown on top, cream belly sometimes tinged red. Rubbery, charcoal grey bill has two obvious nostrils. Broad, flat tail. No visible ears. Webbed feet have 5 toes with long claws. Male has sharp spur, capable of injecting venom, on ankles of hind legs.
Length: ♂ HBT up to 630 mm; ♀ HBT up to 550 mm.
Weight: ♂ 1–3.0 kg; ♀ 0.7–1.8 kg.
Status: Secure.

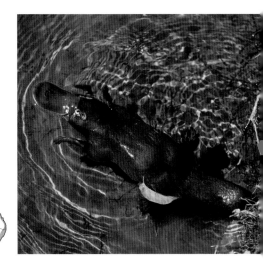

Short-beaked Echidna
Tachyglossus aculeatus

✘ Long-beaked Echidnas *(Zaglosssus bruijni)* and a sub-species of Short-beaked Echidna *(Tachyglossus aculeatus lawesii)* are found in Papua New Guinea.

✘ An Echidna uses the two long claws on its hind foot to groom between its spines.

✘ A Tasmanian Echidna's fur can be longer than its spines.

✘ Echidnas have no teeth.

✘ An Echidna can lift twice its own body weight.

✘ In alpine regions, Echidnas sometimes hibernate during winter.

✘ An Echidna's tongue is 18 cm long.

✘ Male Echidnas have non-venomous spurs on their hind legs.

Short-beaked Echidna

The Short-beaked Echidna, that belongs to the **Tachyglossidae** family, is one of the few native mammals to live in all parts of Australia. It seems equally at home in habitats ranging from tropical rainforest to arid grasslands. An Echidna has a home range, but makes no claim to a permanent den. It prefers to head for the nearest pile of leaves, bush, hollow log or abandoned burrow at dusk.

While its habitat requirements are minimal, the Echidna is a specialist when it comes to food. It feeds exclusively on ants and termites. With more than 1,300 ant species and nearly 350 termite species living in Australia, it has plenty of choice.

An Echidna tracks prey by scent and by using sensors in the tip of its snout to detect electrical impulses in the moving muscles of its prey. It opens up termite and ant nests or underground trails with its claws and snout, then inserts its long, sticky tongue to collect its meal. The insects are crushed between horny plates on the back of the tongue and roof of the mouth. Sometimes, an Echidna will lie on an ant track with its tongue out to trap unsuspecting prey. As it feeds, the Echidna consumes a lot of soil and nest material that pass through the body, forming a large part of its distinctive cylindrical droppings.

A Short-beaked Echidna generally hunts for ants and termites at dawn or dusk, seeking out its prey with its highly sensitive snout.

Breeding

In the winter breeding season a female may find herself being trailed for several days by up to half a dozen males. She selects the most persistent male, who digs a shallow trench under her to avoid being spiked while mating. About two weeks after mating, the female lays a single, 15 millimetre-long, leathery-shelled egg that is incubated in a temporary pouch on her belly for about 10 days at 32°C. Some females prepare a nesting burrow about one metre long during the incubation period; others shelter in dense clumps of vegetation.

After hatching, the baby remains in the pouch until it is covered with short spines. It is then left in a nursery burrow, often found at the base of a termite mound or between tree roots. The mother returns to suckle the baby every one to two days. The young are thought to begin exploring the outside world after three months, but are seldom seen until they are about a year old. During this time they are vulnerable to predators, such as Dingos and goannas.

✘ A female has only one functional ovary.

✘ A young Echidna consumes about 20% of its body weight in milk at each feed.

✘ Echidna milk is pink because it contains a large amount of iron-laden haemoglobin.

✘ A baby Echidna weighs 0.5 g at birth.

✘ The record lifespan of a captive Echidna is 49 years.

Dave Watts, Lochman Transparencies

This juvenile Echidna has yet to grow its spines.

When threatened, an Echidna rolls into a ball to protect its soft belly.

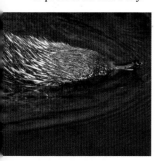

An Echidna will swim to escape danger.

Each spine is formed from a single hair.

Defensive Behaviour

Echidnas are not fighters and rely on their spines and evasive action to escape inexperienced or desperate predators. An Echidna's initial reaction is to freeze and hunch its shoulders to raise its spines. On hard ground it may simply roll up into a spiky ball or it can wedge itself into a nearby crevice or hollow log by raising its spines and spreading its limbs. On soft ground, the Echidna seems to sink below the surface as it digs furiously in a horizontal position. An Echidna cannot throw its spines, but it does shed them once a year.

If surprised on soil, an Echidna can rapidly dig its way under the surface to escape danger.

Finding Echidnas

Echidnas are most active at dawn and dusk. Signs to look for include conical holes in breached ant nests, mating trenches, shed spines and smooth, cylindrical scats. Pigeon-toed front feet and drag marks from the long claws on the backward-facing hind feet leave distinctive tracks.

Location Tips

Found all over Australia in habitats where suitable food and shelter are available.

front foot and print

hind foot and print

Short-beaked Echidna *Tachyglossus aculeatus* (spiny fast-tongue)

The Echidna may not be as intelligent as its competitors and predators, but a specialised diet and a repertoire of escape strategies even the odds when it comes to survival.

Habitat: Any habitat with suitable food and shelter. **Behaviour:** Terrestrial, solitary, active day or night depending on temperature. **Diet:** Ants, termites. **Breeding:** July and August. **Features:** Light to dark brown fur. Dark-tipped cream spines on back and sides. Long, tubular snout. Front foot has 5 toes with broad claws. Long claws on 2nd and 3rd toes of hind foot. Male has ankle spurs. Female has temporary pouch. **Length:** 300–450 mm. **Weight**: 2–7 kg. **Status:** Secure.

MARSUPIALS

Marsupials are the most successful and diverse group of native mammals in Australia. There are about 140 species, and at least one of these amazing animals can be found in almost every part of the continent. They play a range of ecological roles from predatory carnivore to grazing herbivore, just as placental mammals do in other countries.

The way marsupials reproduce sets them apart from other mammals. They are not monotremes because they do not lay eggs and they are not placentals because their newborns are only partially developed.

Marsupials are born in an embryonic state after a brief period of gestation and continue development attached to a teat on the mother's belly.

Marsupial reproduction is just as successful as the placental method and, even though bandicoots and the Koala have a placenta, their newborns are no more advanced than those of other marsupials. While the group gets its name from the word *marsupium,* meaning *pouch,* not all female marsupials have one.

Marsupials were the only mammals, other than primates, to develop opposable digits. These have been retained by tree-climbing species but reduced or lost in the ground dwellers. Many terrestrial marsupials, however, have a unique hind-foot structure with an extra long fourth toe and fused grooming toes. Like monotremes, marsupials have a slower metabolism and smaller brain than placental mammals.

Above: A mob of Eastern Grey Kangaroos alert for danger.
Opposite: The Koala is Australia's most readily recognised mammal.

Yellow-footed Antechinus
Antechinus flavipes

Tasmanian Tiger

At least six species of
Thylacine-like animals
roamed Australia about
10,000 years ago. The
last known Thylacine,
a close relative of
the dasyurids, was
captured in 1933
and died at Hobart
Zoo in 1936. Unable
to compete with
the Dingo, it had
disappeared from the
mainland about 2,000
years earlier. European
settlers in Tasmania
labelled it a sheep-killer
and hunting for
bounty contributed
to its extinction.

© TMAG

Carnivorous Marsupials

There are 56 living species of carnivorous marsupials belonging
to the order **Dasyuromorphia**. While they vary in size and
appearance, they all have squat, triangular heads, and with
the exception of the Kultarr, their front and hind legs are about
equal in length.

Living members of this group are divided into two families.
The **Dasyuridae** family includes the Tasmanian Devil, four
quolls and 50 smaller species. These nocturnal predators
come equipped with an impressive array of sharp teeth that
help them kill and consume their food. The Numbat is the sole
member of the **Myrmecobiidae** family. Unlike its dasyurid
relatives, this termite eater is active during the day and has
small, peg-like teeth.

Michael Morcombe

A Kowari, which is found in Central Australia's stony deserts.
It digs or takes over an existing burrow to shelter during the day.

Quolls

The elegantly furred quoll brings a certain panache to the art of predation. This nocturnal predator strikes with lightning speed, delivering a killer bite to the back of its prey's neck or head. It fastidiously cleans its paws and snout after eating and sometimes leaves the skin of its prey neatly everted.

Quolls are great opportunists. They make the most of food sources on and above the ground. Their varied diet includes fruit, insects, reptiles, birds, rodents and even other marsupial carnivores. They also scavenge and males will challenge females for their catches.

Quolls are efficient nocturnal hunters with keen senses and a dasyurid's characteristic mouthful of teeth: three pairs of lower incisors and four upper pairs are used for tearing, two pairs of canines for stabbing, while blade-like premolars and ridged molars handle the shearing and grinding.

The Spotted-tailed Quoll *Dasyurus maculatus* has an impressive gape

The Eastern Quoll is probably extinct on the mainland, but is common in Tasmania.

✘ Quolls use one or more dens within their home range. These are made in hollow logs, rock crevices and burrows.

✘ Toxoplasmosis, a disease caused by cat parasites, may have decimated quoll populations in the late 1800s.

✘ When threatened, the Western Quoll makes a noise that sounds like its Aboriginal name, "Chuditch".

✘ Quolls living in overlapping home ranges may leave their droppings at a shared "latrine" site.

✘ Northern Quolls sometimes shelter in termite mounds.

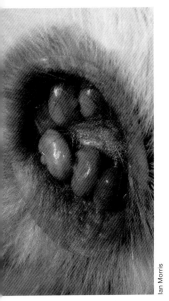

Ian Morris

A litter of newborn
Northern Quolls

✘ A male Spotted-
tailed Quoll will
defend the nursery
den and feed his
mate while she cares
for their offspring.

✘ A female Eastern
Quoll can give birth
to as many as 30
babies, but has only
6 nipples.

✘ Male Northern Quolls
live for 1 or 2 years.
Spotted-tailed Quolls
live for up to 5 years.

✘ Captain James
Cook's 1770
expedition in the
Endeavour collected
quolls and recorded
the word as their
Aboriginal name.

Breeding

Eastern Quolls are no bigger than a grain of rice at birth which
occurs after just two to three weeks in the womb. By the time
they leave the pouch about 10 weeks later, they have barely
opened their eyes and their 20-gram bodies have a scant
covering of fur. They continue to grow in the safety of a nursery
burrow and, when big enough, will cling to the mother's back
as she hunts. A mother will retrieve a youngster that slips off if
she hears its cries.

At about five months, the young are weaned and take up
their independence with little or no parental assistance. This
new generation of quolls may breed a year after their birth.
The stress of their predatory lifestyle and marathon mating
sessions means most will breed for one or two years only.

This litter of captive-bred Eastern Quolls offers researchers
valuable insights on the life-cycle of these remarkable marsupials.

Distribution

Australia's four quoll species were common and widespread at the time of European settlement. Loss of habitat, viruses, predation by Red Foxes, dogs and Feral Cats, as well as competition from introduced animals, have diminished their chances of survival.

The Eastern Quoll was widely distributed from south-east South Australia, throughout Victoria and Tasmania to eastern New South Wales until the late 19th century.

The Western Quoll now occupies only about 5% of its former range, which included all mainland States. It is now considered extinct in the wild on the mainland, although captive-bred individuals have been released in fauna parks and reserves. Eastern and Spotted-tail Quolls are still common in Tasmania, but face an uncertain future should Red Foxes become established on the island.

On the mainland, some populations of Spotted-tail and Northern Quolls are being devastated by the invasion of Cane Toads into their habitat. Quolls that prey on these poisonous toads do not live to hunt again.

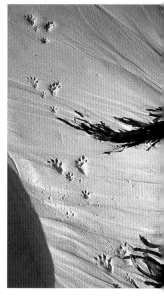

Eastern Quoll tracks on a Tasmanian sand dune.

Finding Quolls

Quolls are active at night, but look for basking quolls on winter days. Check for tracks beside creeks and at the base of trees, rocks and termite mounds. Look for latrine sites with long or twisted cylindrical scats containing fur, feathers, bone or insect skeletons.

Location Tips

→ Cradle Mtn–Lake St Clair NP, Tas
→ Kakadu NP, NT
→ The Hills Forest, WA

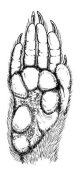

front foot and print of a Spotted-tailed Quoll

hind foot and print of a Spotted-tailed Quoll

Western Quoll *Dasyurus geoffroii* (Geoffroy's hairy-tail)

The Western Quoll, or Chuditch, once claimed Australia's arid and semi-arid regions as its domain. It is now restricted to south-western WA and the total population is estimated to be under 6,000.

Habitat: Eucalypt forest and woodland, mallee shrubland. **Behaviour:** Mostly terrestrial, nocturnal. **Diet:** Insects, reptiles, birds, small mammals. **Breeding:** May to early July, mature by 1 year. **Lifespan:** 3 years.

Features: Sturdy body, brown with white spots above and creamy-white below. Sparsely furred tail with dark feathery tip and no spots. Hind foot has 5 toes and grained sole. Female has pouch and 6 teats. **Length:** ♂ HB 310–400 mm, T 250–350 mm; ♀ HB 260–360 mm, T 210–310 mm. **Weight:** ♂ 700–2200 g; ♀ 600–1120 g. **Status:** Endangered.

Jiri Lochman, Lochman Transparencies

Northern Quoll *Dasyurus hallucatus* (hairy-tail with notable hind foot first digit)

This is the smallest and most aggressive of the four quoll species. It occurs in most habitats across northern Australia, but its populations have been drastically reduced, possibly in part because of the spread of Cane Toads. As with many of the small dasyurids, most of the males die after their first breeding season.

Habitat: Rock outcrops in open eucalypt forest and grassy woodland, human dwellings. **Behaviour:** Mostly arboreal, nocturnal. **Diet:** Invertebrates, reptiles, small mammals, fruit. **Breeding:** Late June, mature by 1 year. **Lifespan:** 1–3 years. **Features:** Grey-brown to brown with large white spots, cream to white below. Pointed snout, large eyes and large

pointed ears. Hind foot has ridged pads and 5 toes. Female has 6–8 teats and develops temporary skinfolds. **Length:** ♂ HB 120–310 mm, T 120–300 mm; ♀ HB 120–300 mm, T 200–300 mm. **Weight:** ♂ 400–900 g; ♀ 300–500 g. **Status:** Endangered.

Spotted-tailed Quoll *Dasyurus maculatus* (spotted hairy-tail)

This agile climber spends most of its time on the ground where it dens in caves, rock crevices and hollow logs. It is the largest carnivorous marsupial on the mainland.

Habitat: Rainforest, eucalypt forest and woodland, coastal heath. **Behaviour:** Partly arboreal, nocturnal but may bask or hunt during day. **Diet:** Insects, birds, medium-sized mammals, carrion. **Breeding:** April to July, mature by 1 year. **Lifespan:** 4–5 years.

Features: Stocky body. Chocolate brown fur with irregular white spots on body and long tail; cream to yellow below. Short face with pointed snout. Hind feet have ridged soles and a clawless opposable first toe for climbing. Female has 6 teats arranged in 2 rows, temporary pouch.
Length: ♂ HB 380–750 mm, T 370–550 mm; ♀ HB 350–450 mm, T 340–420 mm.
Weight: ♂ up to 7 kg; ♀ up to 4 kg.
Status: Vulnerable in Tas and SE Aust; endangered in north Qld.

Eastern Quoll *Dasyurus viverrinus* (ferret-like hairy-tail)

Once widespread in south-east mainland Australia, there have been no recorded mainland sightings of this swift and graceful predator since 1963. The species is still common in Tasmania. While females hunt near their dens, males will travel up to 1 km in search of prey.

Habitat: Eucalypt forest, scrub, heath, farmland. **Behaviour:** Mostly terrestrial, solitary, nocturnal. **Diet:** Insects, ground-nesting birds, small mammals, carrion, grass, fruit.
Breeding: May to early July, mature at 11 months. **Lifespan:** Up to 5 years.
Features: Thick, soft fur with irregular white spots on back and sides. Can be black with brown belly or fawn with white belly. Tail has no spots. Four toes on hind foot. Large rounded ears. Female has 6 teats, develops temporary skinfolds. **Length:** ♂ HB 320–450 mm, T 200–280 mm; ♀ HB 280–400 mm, T 170–240 mm. **Weight:** ♂ 900–2000 g; ♀ 700–1100 g. **Status:** Secure in Tas, endangered on mainland.

Tasmanian Devils
Sarcophilus harrisii

Tasmanian Devil

With its blood-curdling scream and bone-crushing jaws, the Tasmanian Devil looks and sounds like a ferocious predator. But Australia's largest and most famous marsupial carnivore has trouble catching anything larger than insects or animals the size of a rat. It is an expert scavenger that would rather feed on carrion or steal prey from its smaller relatives, the quolls.

When more than one Devil scents out the same carcass, they champ, growl and shriek at one another. Once the ritualised squabbling is out of the way, they settle down to a shared meal.

A Devil's powerful jaws and sharp teeth make short work of large mammal carcasses. A thick wombat skull may defeat it, but it will hold a kangaroo leg bone in its paws and chomp away as if eating a carrot. The only evidence of its nocturnal feasts is usually some fur and the intestines which it delicately removes from the stomach cavity.

✘ Devils live up to 8 years in captivity.

✘ Lymphatic cancer has wiped out a third of the total population of Tasmanian Devils since 1995.

✘ The Tasmanian Devil was hunted almost to extinction. It was not protected until June 1941.

✘ A Tasmanian Devil's ears turn deep red when it is agitated.

✘ A Devil's bounding run gives it a top speed of about 13 km/h.

This Tasmanian Devil displays its powerful jaws and sharp teeth.

A Devil's Playground

Just over 400 years ago Tasmanian Devils joined Thylacines, or Tasmanian Tigers, as exiles in Tasmania. Subsequent European settlement of the island not only provided Devils with new food sources and habitats, but also elevated them to the role of top native carnivore by contributing to the extinction of the Thylacine.

They are now widespread; however, their future is not guaranteed. Predation and competition from introduced animals, extermination by people who regard them as a pest species, and disease may see the Tasmanian Devil follow the Thylacine's path to extinction.

Tasmanian Devils have home ranges of 10–20 hectares. Although territories overlap, they live and hunt alone. Devils follow well-worn trails through the bush as they search for food between dusk and dawn. They can travel up to 16 kilometres in a night when food is scarce.

During the day they retreat to dens in dense bush, hollow logs, caves or, often, a deserted wombat burrow. Devils are not territorial, except near a breeding den.

A Tasmanian Devil pauses in the undergrowth during a nocturnal foray.

Young Tasmanian Devils practise the skills needed to compete for food.

A mother and her young share a meal.

Breeding

A female Tasmanian Devil begins breeding at two years of age. She bears two young in her first season and then three or four annually for the next three years. Like most dasyurids, she produces more babies than her four nipples can accommodate.

Tasmanian Devils mate in March and the young are born a month later. They remain in their mother's backward-facing pouch for 15 weeks and then are left in a den. By October the cubs are weaned and have begun following their mother, sometimes catching a lift on her back.

Young Tasmanian Devils indulge in noisy, boisterous play. They wrestle and tumble with each other, snapping and gaping their jaws in imitation of adults guarding food. They also are very agile and can scramble up sloping branches in search of roosting birds.

A pair of young Tasmanian Devils rest between bouts of play and wrestling.

Finding Devils

During the day look for foraging trails, burrow entrances, tracks and droppings. The broken or twisted cylindrical scats are grey, smelly and contain bone fragments and fur. The Devil's awkward gait leaves a distinctive one-two-one pattern of squarish paw prints. At night, listen for calls or wait quietly near fresh roadkill.

Location Tips

→ Cradle Mtn–Lake St Clair NP
→ Freycinet NP
→ Mt William NP

front foot
and print

hind foot
and print

Tasmanian Devil *Sarcophilus harrisii* (Harris's flesh-lover)

Australia's largest carnivorous marsupial lives only in Tasmania. Once widespread on the mainland, the arrival and spread of the Dingo and climate change may have contributed to its extinction there.

Habitat: All habitats – eucalypt forest, woodlands, heath and farmland. **Behaviour:** Terrestrial, nocturnal. **Diet:** Insects, mammals up to wombat size, carrion. **Breeding:** March, females mature at 2 years. **Lifespan:** About 6 years. **Features:** Compact, muscular body with short, broad head and small eyes. Black with white streak across chest, sometimes white patch on rump. Sparsely furred snout and ears. 5 toes on front foot; 4 toes on long hind foot. Male larger with broader head and thicker neck. Female has 4 teats and a pouch. **Length:** ♂ HB 650 mm, T 260 mm; ♀ HB 570 mm; T 245 mm. **Weight:** ♂ 9 kg, ♀ 7 kg. **Status:** Secure.

Brush-tailed Phascogale
Phascogale tapoatafa

✗ Very small dasyurid females ovulate only once a year because they don't have the energy required to ovulate more often.

✗ Brown Antechinus males die at the end of their 2-week mating season.

✗ The female Fawn Antechinus may give birth to 16 young but has only 10 nipples.

✗ The female Sandstone Pseudantechinus has no pouch.

✗ The tiny Long-tailed Planigale, weighing 4 g, is the world's smallest marsupial and second smallest mammal.

✗ A newborn Kowari is 3 mm long.

✗ Fat-tailed Dunnarts huddle together in nests to keep warm in winter.

Small Dasyurids

Within Australia's forests, woodlands and deserts live 50 species of flesh-eating marsupials renowned for their ferocity and voracious appetites. They hunt under cover of darkness, relying on speed and agility to hunt and kill prey. These small, secretive members of the **Dasyuridae** family weigh between four and 300 grams. Their size belies their aggressive nature and these feisty, pocket-sized predators often take on prey larger than themselves. When threatened, they respond with bared teeth, hisses, growls and shrieks.

Strong legs and long hind feet with ridged soles give these predators the power and traction they need when running or climbing. Tree-dwelling species also have a thumb-like inner toe on each hind foot for extra grip.

Aridland Hunters

Desert-dwelling marsupial carnivores have many features and strategies for staying alive in difficult conditions. They are most active at night and avoid the heat of the day by sheltering in burrows, rock crevices and cracks in the ground. They can slow down their metabolism to save energy when temperatures are extreme. Some produce concentrated urine to reduce water loss. When food is scarce, they can call on stored body fats, and delay breeding. Their ability to produce and raise young quickly during brief wet spells gives them an advantage over competitors.

A female Brush-tailed Phascogale demonstrates her kind's preference for a tree hollow with a small entrance as a nursery.

Breeding

Small marsupial carnivores are prolific breeders. The females give birth to more young than their nipples can accommodate and some produce more than one litter per season. Such fecundity has its price and few live more than two to three years.

The males of several antechinus and phascogale species do not survive beyond their first breeding season. They use enormous amounts of energy pursuing females, fighting other males and engaging in mating sessions lasting up to 12 hours. Their frenetic sexual behaviour causes their immune systems to break down and they die before their offspring are born.

It is first in, first served when a mother has more babies than nipples. The blind and furless newborns that succeed in finding a nipple remain attached for about five weeks. Those not protected by a pouch risk being dislodged as the mother forages for enough food to keep up her milk supply.

When they are too big to be dragged beneath her belly, the young are left in a nest or cling to their mother's back. They are weaned within three to five months and most are sexually mature by 10 months.

Tiny, hairless young cluster on a female dasyurid's teats.

✘ The Mulgara gets all the water it needs from the spiders, insects and rodents it eats.

✘ The bristles on the Hairy-footed Dunnart's feet give traction on sand.

Jiri Lochman, Lochman Transparencies

Two juvenile Mulgaras observe their mother's successful hunting technique.

Mulgara *Dasycercus cristicauda* (crest-tailed hairy-tail)

Mulgaras are fast, efficient hunters that move with a bounding gait. They dig burrows with tunnels, shafts and pop-up holes in and between sand dunes. The Mulgara produces a small amount of highly concentrated urine, allowing it to survive on water obtained from its prey.

Habitat: Inland sandy deserts. **Behaviour:** Terrestrial, solitary, mostly nocturnal. **Diet:** Insects, spiders, scorpions, small vertebrates. **Breeding:** Mid May to October. Mature at 10–11 months.

Lifespan: Up to 7 years.

Features: Fine, soft fur is light sandy brown above, greyish white below. Tail has reddish base and black crest. Rounded ears are sparsely furred. Front and hind feet have 5 toes. Female has pouch and 8 teats.

Length: ♂ HB 125–220 mm, T 75–125 mm; ♀ HB 125–170 mm, T 75–100 mm.

Weight: ♂ 75–170 g; ♀ 60–95 g.

Status: Vulnerable.

Ian Morris

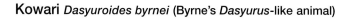

Kowari *Dasyuroides byrnei* (Byrne's *Dasyurus*-like animal)

These solitary hunters, male and female, use urine and scent glands on their chests to mark their burrows and home ranges. They chatter and hiss at interlopers, switching their tails and raising one front foot as a threat.

Habitat: Gibber plains. **Behaviour:** Terrestrial, solitary, nocturnal. **Diet:** Insects, small vertebrates, carrion. **Breeding:** May through December. May produce two litters per season. Mature at 9 months. **Features:** Light grey-brown to sandy brown above and greyish white below. Eyes are large. Snout and thin ears are sparsely furred. Black, bottlebrush tail-tip. 4 toes on hind foot. Female develops skinfolds and has 6–7 teats. **Length:** ♂ HB 140–180 mm, T 110–140 mm; ♀ HB 135–160 mm, T 110–130 mm.

Weight: ♂ 85–140 g; ♀ 70–105 g.

Status: Vulnerable.

Southern Dibbler *Parantechinus apicalis* (pointed *Antechinus*-like animal)

The Southern Dibbler was first discovered in 1884 and was not seen again until 1967. Thriving populations exist on Boullanger and Whitlock Islands, but mainland distribution seems limited to Fitzgerald River and Torndirrup National Parks, Western Australia.

Habitat: Coastal heath. **Behaviour:** Partly arboreal, nocturnal.
Diet: Insects, possibly nectar. **Breeding:** Mates in March. Mature at 10–11 months.
Lifespan: 1–3 years. Most males die after their first breeding season.
Features: Coarse fur, grey-brown flecked with white above, greyish white below, sides tinged yellow. White ring around eye. Short, hairy, tapered tail. 5 toes on hind foot. Female has shallow pouch and 8 teats.
Length: ♂ HB 145 mm,
T 105–115 mm;
♀ HB 140 mm, T 95 mm.
Weight: ♂ 60–100 g;
♀ 40–75 g.
Status: Endangered.

Michael Morcombe

Sandstone Pseudantechinus *Pseudantechinus bilarni* (Bill Harney's false-*Antechinus*)

Although well known to Arnhem Land Aborigines, this marsupial first came to scientific attention in 1948. Its high metabolic rate often drives it from shelter in search of late afternoon snacks.

Habitats: Sandstone escarpments, prefers boulder slopes with grassy eucalypt forest, may move to monsoon forest in dry season. **Behaviour:** Terrestrial, carnivorous, mostly nocturnal. **Diet:** Insects and other small invertebrates. **Breeding:** Late June to early July. Mature at 12 months. **Lifespan:** 1–3 years. About 75% die after the first breeding season. **Features:** Grey-brown above and pale grey below. Forehead is marked with darker fur. Pointed snout is almost hairless. Has reddish patches behind large, thin ears. Tail is long, slender and scaly. Female has 6 teats and no pouch.
Length: ♂ HB 90–115 mm,
T 90–125 mm;
♀ HB 90–115 mm, T 90–120 mm.
Weight: ♂ 20–40 g; ♀ 15–35 g.
Status: Secure.

Belinda Wright

Fat-tailed Pseudantechinus
Pseudantechinus macdonnellensis (MacDonnell Ranges false-*Antechinus*)

This marsupial shelters in crevices or termite mounds, and comes out to bask on winter days. Fat is stored in the base of its short tail when insect prey is plentiful.

Habitat: Sparsely vegetated aridland with rocky outcrops.

Behaviour: Terrestrial, mostly nocturnal.
Diet: Insects and other small invertebrates.
Breeding: July through September. Mature by 12 months.
Features: Greyish brown fur with chestnut patches behind large ears. Large eyes and broad hind feet. Short tail. Female has 6 teats and develops temporary skinfolds.
Length: ♂ HB 95–105 mm, T 75–80 mm; ♀ HB 95–105 mm; T 75–85 mm.

Weight: ♂ 25–45 g; ♀ 20–40 g.
Status: Secure.

Ian Morris

Fawn Antechinus *Antechinus bellus* (beautiful hedgehog-equivalent)

The Fawn Antechinus is common but rarely seen in its northern tropical habitat. It is one of the largest antechinus species and relies on tree and log hollows for shelter.

Habitat: Open eucalypt forest and woodland with grassy or shrubby undergrowth.
Behaviour: Shelters and hunts on the ground and in trees, nocturnal.

Diet: Insects. **Breeding:** Late August. Up to 10 young, which are weaned in January.
Lifespan: Males die after first breeding season. **Features:** Pale to medium grey fur, sometimes with brownish tinge; belly cream to pale grey. Chin and paws white. Tail is shorter than combined head and body length. Female has 10 teats.
Length: ♂ HB 121–148 mm, T 105–126 mm; ♀ HB 110–130 mm, T 93–110 mm.
Weight: ♂ 42–66 g; ♀ 26–41 g.
Status: Common.

Ian Morris

Yellow-footed Antechinus
Antechinus flavipes (yellow-footed hedgehog-equivalent)

These inquisitive creatures dart over the ground, bulldozing through leaf litter and pouncing on prey. They run along the underside of branches when hunting in trees.

Habitat: Ranges from rainforest to mulga woodland and suburban gardens.
Behaviour: Arboreal and terrestrial, gregarious, nocturnal. **Diet:** Insects, small birds, rodents, flowers, nectar.
Breeding: Late winter to spring.
Lifespan: Males die after mating.
Features: Slate grey head with white-ringed eyes grading to orange-brown sides, rump, belly and feet. Throat and chest white. Tail has black tip. Female has 8 nipples and develops temporary skinfolds.

Length: ♂ HB 93–165 mm, T 70–151 mm; ♀ HB 86–127 mm, T 65–107 mm.
Weight: ♂ 26–79 g; ♀ 21–52 g.
Status: Secure.

Brush-tailed Phascogale
Phascogale tapoatafa (pouched-weasel + Aboriginal name)

Sharp claws and hind feet that can rotate 180° make this dasyurid a nimble climber. These social creatures often share nests and alert others to danger by tapping on branches.

Habitat: Open eucalypt woodland with sparse undergrowth.
Behaviour: Mostly arboreal, gregarious, nocturnal.
Diet: Insects, spiders, small vertebrates, nectar. **Breeding:** Mid May–early June. Mature by 11 months. **Lifespan:** 1–3 years. Males die after mating.
Features: Grey fur flecked with black on head, back and sides; cream below. Large ears and eyes. Dark stripe down centre of face. Black, bottlebrush tail with hairs up to 40 mm long. Short fifth toe on hind foot. Female has 8 teats and develops temporary skinfolds.

Length: ♂ HB 160–261 mm, T 175–234 mm; ♀ HB 148–223 mm, T 160–226 mm.
Weight: ♂ 175–311 g; ♀ 106–212 g.
Status: Secure. Vulnerable in Vic.

Common Planigale *Planigale maculata* (spotted flat-weasel)

This planigale is best known for it tenacious grip and fearless attacks on insects larger than itself. It shelters in crevices, under rocks and in hollow logs.

Habitat: Rainforest, eucalypt forest, grassland, marshes, rocky outcrops, suburban gardens.

Behaviour: Mostly terrestrial, nocturnal. **Diet:** Insects. **Breeding:** Late spring and summer in the east, all year elsewhere. **Features:** Cinnamon to grey-brown fur sometimes speckled with white. Pale underbelly and white chin. Large, notched ears. Thin tail is shorter than head and body. Female has pouch and 8–12 nipples. **Length:** ♂ HB 70–100 mm, T 61–95 mm; ♀ HB 71–87 mm, T 64–82 mm. **Weight:** ♂ 6–22 g; ♀ 7–15 g. **Status:** Secure.

Ian Morris

Kultarr *Antechinomys laniger* (woolly *Antechinus*-mouse)

Long hind legs and a bounding gait give the Kultarr extra manoeuvrability. Recognisable calls allow a mother to retrieve unweaned young that stray or fall from her back.

Habitat: Stone and sand plains in grassland, shrubland or woodland. **Behaviour:** Terrestrial, solitary, nocturnal. **Diet:** Insects, spiders. **Breeding:** July to February. Can produce 2 litters per season. Mature at 8 months. **Features:** Fawn-grey to sandy brown above, white below. Dark stripe from crown to nose. Large ears. Protruding eyes with dark rings. Long, thin tail with dark brush. Very long hind foot with 4 toes. Female has 6–8 teats and temporary skinfolds.

Length: ♂ HB 80–100 mm, T 100–150 mm; ♀ HB 70–95 mm, T 100–140 mm. **Weight:** ♂ 30 g; ♀ 20 g. **Status:** Secure.

Michael Morcombe

Fat-tailed Dunnart *Sminthopsis crassicaudata* (fat-tailed mouse-like animal)

In cold weather, Fat-tailed Dunnarts will huddle together in communal nests. Fat stored in the tail becomes a source of energy when food is scarce.

Habitat: Wide range from coastal areas to arid inland – woodland, grassland, shrubland, farmland and gibber plains.

Behaviour: Terrestrial, nocturnal.

Diet: Invertebrates.

Breeding: July to February. May produce 2 litters per season.

Features: Greyish brown above, light grey to white below. Large ears. Round, protruding eyes. Short, fat tail. Hind foot has grainy, raised pads. Female has pouch and 8–10 teats.

Length: HB 60–90 mm; T 40–70 mm.

Weight: 10–20 g.

Status: Secure.

Ian Morris

Red-cheeked Dunnart *Sminthopsis virginiae* (Virginia's mouse-like animal)

The Red-cheeked Dunnart proved elusive after it was discovered in 1847, and every time it was rediscovered it was given a new name. It is found in Australia's north and New Guinea.

Habitat: Tropical savanna woodland near creeks and billabongs.

Behaviour: Terrestrial, solitary, nocturnal.

Diet: Insects, small reptiles.

Breeding: All year. Mature at 4 to 6 months.

Features: Spiky, dark grey fur flecked with white, white to cream below. Red cheeks. Dark stripe from forehead to nose. Eyes and ears are large and round. Thin tail almost furless. Hind foot has 4 long toes and 1 short inner toe. Female has pouch and 8 teats.

Length: ♂ HB 96–135 mm, T 100–135 mm; ♀ HB 90–133 mm; T 90–122 mm.

Weight: ♂ 31–58 g; ♀ 18–34 g.

Status: Secure.

Ian Morris

Numbat *Myrmecobius fasciatus*

Numbat

A marsupial carnivore armed with more teeth than any other native land mammal is a fearsome prospect for any prey. But 25 pairs of teeth are of little use when most of them lie below the gum line. A 100 millimetre-long tongue that moves faster than the human eye can see is, however, a formidable weapon for a predator that feeds exclusively on termites. The Numbat sniffs out its prey, then scratches open their log nests or shallow underground runways. Its sticky, flickering tongue traps the termites and it swallows them whole along with any ants that might take advantage of the feeding opportunity the Numbat's activity offers. Numbats hunt during the day when termites are most active. In winter, both termites and Numbats remain in their nests on cold mornings. When summer temperatures drive termites deeper underground, Numbats bide their time in shady retreats.

✘ A Numbat's tongue is about half as long as its head and body combined.

✘ Fewer than 2,000 Numbats are thought to survive in the wild.

✘ Numbats line their nests with shredded bark and leaves.

✘ The Numbat is Western Australia's faunal emblem.

✘ Numbats will not share their territories with members of the same sex.

✘ A Numbat eats up to 20,000 termites a day.

✘ Land clearing and foxes are the biggest threats to Numbats' survival.

Sharp claws and textured foot pads provide traction for the tree-climbing Numbat.

Habitat

The Numbat is the only living member of the **Myrmecobiidae** family. At the time of European settlement it could be found in woodlands and forests across southern Australia to western New South Wales. It is now confined to isolated pockets of Jarrah and Wandoo forest in the south-west. These eucalypt forests provide old trees, fallen timber and shrubby undergrowth that shelter Numbats and feed termites.

While foraging, the Numbat moves along at a brisk trot, tail raised in a bristling arc above its back. It stops frequently to stand and sniff the air or scrabble in leaf litter and rotting logs. It takes a lot of termites to support such a high energy animal and a Numbat's territory can range from 25 to 50 hectares. It maintains several nests in logs, burrows and tree hollows within its home range and beds down in the nearest one at dusk.

Breeding

Breeding is a fairly synchronised event for Numbats. The January mating season is brief and a female only has a 48-hour window of opportunity to conceive. Most of the young are born in late January and early February after 14 days' gestation. The female Numbat has no pouch and her long belly hairs offer minimal protection to her under-developed babies.

By late July the young no longer need to suckle constantly and they are left in a nursery chamber at the end of a burrow one to two metres long. They begin exploring the outside world in September and within a few weeks have learned to feed themselves. At the age of 10 months, they leave home to find their own territories.

A tree hollow makes an effective Numbat shelter.

Michael Morcombe

A female Numbat has no pouch to protect her young.

The Numbat's cryptic colouring helps it blend into the light and shadow of its home on the forest floor.

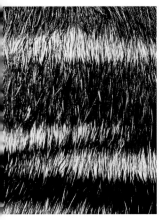

A detail of the Numbat's distinctive markings.

Defensive Behaviour

The Numbat relies on camouflage to deceive the eyes and minds of its daytime predators. The Numbat's colours and stripes break up its body outline and help it blend into its open forest habitat.

When standing still, the Numbat becomes part of a confusing image of light and shadow. When a Numbat runs, its flashing white stripes create a flicker effect that dazzles the eye and is difficult to process. While a predator's other senses are overriding its visual confusion, the Numbat may have just enough time to escape to a nearby bolthole.

A cornered Numbat can only hope that its dark eye stripes will make its head a less conspicuous target than its bushy tail. A predator that goes for the tail may be left with a mouthful of hair as the rest of its dinner heads off in the opposite direction.

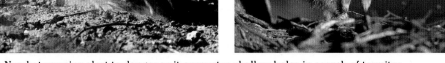

A Numbat remains alert to danger as it excavates shallow holes in search of termites.

Finding Numbats

Location Tips

Try a late afternoon walk in a Wandoo or Jarrah forest. Check the ground for shallow, funnel-shaped holes. Look for dark, shiny cylindrical droppings on logs. Tracks are similar to the Western Quoll, but the front foot has longer claws and the hind foot has only 4 toes.

→ Dryandra State Forest, WA
→ Perup Forest, WA
→ Dragon Rocks Nature Reserve, WA
→ Boyagin Nature Reserve, WA

hind foot and print

front foot and print

Numbat *Myrmecobius fasciatus* (banded feeder-on-ants)

Numbats are being reintroduced to suitable habitats in nature reserves and national parks where control programs reduce the threat of feral predators.

Habitat: Eucalypt forest and woodland with shrubby undergrowth.
Behaviour: Mostly terrestrial, territorial, solitary, diurnal. **Diet:** Termites. **Breeding:** January. Females mature at 1 year, males at 2 years. **Lifespan:** 2–3 years. **Features:** Coarse, reddish brown fur with darker, sometimes black rump; pale below. 4–11 transverse white stripes between shoulders and base of tail. Narrow head with large ears. White eyebrows and white patch below dark eye stripe running from nose to ear. Bushy tail with long hairs. Hind foot has 4 toes. Female has 4 teats and no pouch.
Length: ♂ HB 200–274 mm, T 164–210 mm; ♀ HB 200–272 mm, T 161–195 mm.
Weight: ♂ 300–715 g; ♀ 320–678 g.
Status: Vulnerable.

✘ A marsupial mole's ears are just small holes surrounded by dense hair.

✘ The Northern Marsupial Mole is smaller than the southern species and is cinnamon in colour.

✘ Marsupial moles travel 100–200 mm below the surface, but may suddenly "dive" 2.5 m.

✘ In captivity, they often feed above ground.

✘ Some males have a rudimentary pouch.

✘ Marsupial mole fossils 15–20 million years old have been found in north-west Queensland.

Marsupial Moles

Marsupial moles are unusual Australian mammals that have had scientists puzzling over how to classify them since 1888. It was decided they were different enough from other marsupial groups to warrant their own classification order called **Notoryctemorphia**, and two species of the genus *Notoryctes*, *N. typhlops* and *N. caurinus*, have been identified so far.

These blind, desert-dwelling carnivores spend most of their time tunnelling underground in search of insect larvae. Their bodies are well suited to a burrowing lifestyle with two large spade-like front claws and a horny shield to protect the snout. Fine fur, a short, tapered tail and lack of external ears streamline the body.

A marsupial mole seems to swim through the sand – as it moves forward, the tunnel fills behind it. It usually digs horizontal tunnels 10–20 centimetres below the surface, although it has been known to sink vertical shafts exceeding depths of two metres. It sleeps standing up with its back arched against the tunnel roof so it does not suffocate. Sinuous tracks of parallel grooves are the only signs of its brief above-ground forays that may occur after rain.

Southern Marsupial Mole *Notoryctes typhlops* (blind southern-digger)

Marsupial moles burrow in sand dunes, interdune flats and river flats. Aboriginal people of central Australia, who call the mole *Itjaritjari*, traded their pelts to settlers and camel drivers.

Habitat: Sandy deserts with spinifex or mulga. **Behaviour:** Terrestrial, solitary. **Diet:** Insects. **Breeding:** Unknown. **Features:** Soft, silky fur varies from yellowish white to deep gold. Pad of leathery skin on snout. Short, scaly, knobbed tail. 5 toes on each foot, 2 on front feet modified for digging. Female has 2 teats and backward-opening pouch. **Length:** HB 121–159 mm, T 21–26 mm. **Weight:** 40–70 g. **Status:** Endangered.

Stan Breeden

Bruce Thomson, ANTPhoto.com

Bruce Thomson, ANTPhoto.com

Bilby *Macrotis lagotis*

Bandicoots and the Bilby

Bandicoots and the Bilby belong to the order **Peramelemorphia** which is divided into two families. The **Peramelidae** family includes short-eared bandicoots and the Bilby. The rainforest dwelling Rufous Spiny Bandicoot is the only Australian member of the **Peroryctidae** family.

Bandicoots are terrestrial marsupials that rely on thick undergrowth of shrubs and grasses for food and shelter. They spend the day in camouflaged nests of leaf litter scraped into a pile in a shallow depression. Sometimes a layer of soil is kicked over the top for waterproofing.

They emerge at night to forage over territories ranging from one to six hectares. Insects, worms and other invertebrates are a bandicoot's preferred foods, but it also eats fruit and fleshy plant roots. It locates underground food by smell and leaves distinctive 10 centimetre-deep, cone-shaped holes where it digs.

✘ In Queensland, a 25 km^2 enclosure allows the Bilby, whose populations were dangerously low, to breed in an area free of stock and feral animals.

A Missing Link?

Some scientists believe bandicoots are an evolutionary link between marsupial carnivores and herbivores. A bandicoot has the teeth of a typical dasyurid carnivore, except its incisors are flat-edged and point slightly outwards to suit its mixed diet. The hind legs and feet, however, resemble those of a plant-eating macropod. Like kangaroos, the hind foot has an extra long fourth toe and joined second and third toes that are used for grooming. The bandicoot has a bounding gait and its strong leg muscles allow it to bounce into the air and leap distances of up to a metre.

Below: Northern Brown Bandicoot

Breeding

Bandicoots are aggressive, territorial animals. When paths cross, there is a brief exchange of hisses, grunts and squeals, a bit of pouncing and chasing, then each goes its separate way.

Mating encounters are equally brief; however, breeding seasons are long and a female may produce two or three litters a year. Unlike most other marsupials, bandicoots have rudimentary placentas. The placental cords provide attachment to the womb for the embryonic young, but there is no transfer of nutrients and wastes.

Bandicoots have the shortest gestation period of any mammal – 12.5 days. Usually two or three young are carried in the female's backward-opening pouch for about seven weeks. A nursing female can become pregnant during the week it takes to wean her young. She gives birth to another litter within days of the previous brood leaving to find their own territories.

✘ Australia has 8 living species of bandicoots including the Bilby.

✘ Male bandicoots are larger and more aggressive than females.

✘ Bandicoots are not rodents even though their name is derived from an Indonesian word for rat.

✘ Bandicoots have an average lifespan of 3 years.

✘ Some bandicoot species excavate suburban lawns to feed on the black beetle and beetle larvae (known as curl grubs) which cause die-back.

✘ The Western Barred Bandicoot is extinct on the mainland.

✘ A newborn Long-nosed Bandicoot weighs 0.25 g and is about 13 mm long.

✘ A female has eight nipples but only bears two to three young per litter.

✘ Bandicoots breed in winter, spring and summer. In northern regions they may breed throughout the year.

Ian Morris

Insects and other arthropods are the main source of food for the Long-nosed Bandicoot.

Burrowing Bilbies

The Bilby is the only Australian species of bandicoot that makes underground shelters. A Bilby burrow spirals downwards one to two metres and can be up to three metres long. The single entrance is usually concealed at the base of a termite mound, grass clump or shrub. A Bilby maintains several burrows where it can shelter during the day.

These energetic excavators usually begin foraging around midnight. They have poor vision, but a keen sense of smell leads them to food. With tails aloft and noses to the ground, they lick up grass and acacia seeds and unearth insects, spiders, bulbs and fungi. They will take on small mammals and lizards when other food is scarce.

Bilbies live alone or in small family groups and forage within their home ranges. In ideal conditions, a square kilometre of habitat can support up to 16 Bilbies. When territories overlap, males and females establish separate pecking orders. A male's eligibility to mate depends on his rank in the hierarchy. Breeding also depends on the availability of food, even though females can mate throughout the year. In a good year, a female may produce four litters of one to two young.

Ian Morris

Dalgyte, Ninu and *Walpatjirri* are among the names Aborigines have given the Bilby.

✘ The Bilby is Australia's largest bandicoot.

✘ The Lesser Bilby hasn't been seen since 1931 and is presumed extinct.

✘ Aborigines hunted Bilbies for food and used their tails for ceremonial purposes.

✘ Bilby bush tucker includes witchetty grubs, Honeypot Ants, termites and wild onion bulbs.

✘ A Bilby may have up to 12 burrows within its home range.

The Bilby makes burrows and digs for food with the help of three stout, curved claws on each front foot.

Distribution

In the 1920s, Bilbies were common in the arid and semi-arid woodland and grassland that covered 70% of mainland Australia. Today there are only scattered populations in the central and western deserts and a small area of Queensland's channel country.

Within Currawinya National Park in south-west Queensland, a fence, built by volunteers with money from the Save the Bilby Fund, encloses an area where Bilbies can live and breed without being threatened by feral predators.

As a species, the Bilby struggles against habitat change and introduced animals, but it has an incredible ability to survive in one of Australia's harshest and most unforgiving environments. Its silky fur and deep burrows insulate the Bilby from extreme temperatures. It does not need to drink and, instead of sweating out precious moisture, it seems that its large thin ears packed with blood vessels allow excess body heat to escape.

Opportunistic breeding and a rigid social structure help balance population numbers with food supply. When food becomes scarce during lengthy dry periods, Bilbies abandon their burrows and move to a new territory.

✖ Foxes, Feral Cats, Dingos and owls prey on Bilbies.

✖ Bilbies make cone-shaped holes up to 25 cm deep when digging up food.

✖ A female Bilby has 8 nipples but only raises 1 or 2 babies per litter.

✖ Young Bilbies spend 75 to 80 days in their mother's backward-opening pouch.

✖ At night, a female leaves her young in the burrow, returning at intervals to feed them.

Finding Bandicoots

Look on the ground for domed piles of leaf litter used as nests and narrow, 10-cm-deep, conical excavations. Scats are brown or black smooth cylindrical pellets containing soil, plant fibres and insect remains. Front-foot prints usually show only 3 toes. The Bilby's hind-foot prints are slightly pigeon-toed, its scats can be tinged red and its burrow entrances may be found at the base of termite mounds and grass tussocks.

Location Tips

→ Freycinet NP, Tas
→ Fitzgerald River NP, WA
→ Kakadu NP, NT
→ Bilby: Currawinya NP, Qld

front foot and print of Long-nosed Bandicoot

hind foot and print of Long-nosed Bandicoot

Golden Bandicoot *Isoodon auratus* (golden equal-tooth)

A Golden Bandicoot can cover up to 10 hectares a night while foraging. While it is the most common mammal on Barrow Island, off the coast of Western Australia, it is restricted to isolated populations on the mainland.

Habitat: Arid and semi-arid grassland and grassy woodland, monsoon forest.
Behaviour: Terrestrial, territorial, solitary, nocturnal. **Diet:** Insects, plant roots and tubers, small reptiles and mammals. **Lifespan:** About 3 years. **Breeding:** All year, peaking in

summer and August. More than 1 litter per year. Usually 2 young per litter.
Features: Black-flecked, golden brown guard hairs over grey underfur. White belly. Rounded ears. Long, slender tail. Female has 8 teats and rear-opening pouch. **Length:** HB 190–295 mm, T 84–121 mm. **Weight:** 250–670 g. **Status:** Vulnerable.

Ian Morris

Northern Brown Bandicoot *Isoodon macrourus* (long-tailed equal-tooth)

Males are larger and more aggressive than the females, and use scent glands behind their ears to mark their territories. They often lose their tails in territorial disputes.

Habitat: Forest, woodland, grassland, suburban gardens.
Behaviour: Terrestrial, territorial, solitary, nocturnal. **Diet:** Insects, spiders, worms, fruit, grass seeds. **Breeding:** August to April, all year in south-east Queensland. 1–2 litters per

season. Females mature at 3–4 months.
Lifespan: About 3 years.
Features: Coarse, dark brown fur speckled with black; belly is greyish white. Small, pointed ears and short, pointed tail. Female has 8 teats and rear-opening pouch.
Length: ♂ HB 300–470 mm, T 90–215 mm; ♀ HB 300–410 mm; T 80–185 mm. **Weight:** ♂ 500–3100 g; ♀ 500–1700 g. **Status:** Secure.

Southern Brown Bandicoot *Isoodon obesulus* (rather fat equal-tooth)

The Southern Brown Bandicoot prefers habitats with sandy soils and scrubby undergrowth where occasional fires renew plant and insect food sources. It is territorial and aggressively defends its two to seven hectare home range.

Habitat: Dry eucalypt forest, woodland, shrubland. **Behaviour:** Terrestrial, territorial, solitary, nocturnal. **Diet:** Insects, other invertebrates, fungi, plant roots. **Breeding:** Winter and summer. 2–3 litters per season. Females mature at 3–4 months. **Lifespan:** About 3 years. **Features:** Solid body with hunched posture. Brownish grey fur flecked with yellow and brown, creamy white below. Bristly guard hairs cover upper body. Short, pointed tail and upper surface of hind feet usually dark brown. Small, rounded ears. Female has 8 teats and rear-opening pouch. **Length:** ♂ HB 300–360 mm, T 90–140 mm; ♀ HB 280–330 mm; T 90–140 mm.
Weight: ♂ 500–1600 g; ♀ 400–1100 g.
Status: Endangered on mainland.

Western Barred Bandicoot
Perameles bougainville (Bougainville's pouched-badger)

The Western Barred Bandicoot is found only on Bernier and Dorre Islands off the WA coast. Prior to European settlement it existed in a variety of habitats across southern Australia. It occupies a nest of leaves in a scrape under a shrub during the day.

Habitat: Coastal scrub and grassland. **Behaviour:** Terrestrial, territorial, solitary, nocturnal. **Diet:** Insects and other small animals, plant roots, leaves and seeds. **Breeding:** April to October. More than 1 litter per season. Usually 2 young per litter. **Lifespan:** About 3 years. **Features:** Light grey to greyish-brown above with 2–3 pale stripes on rump. Underside and feet are white. Large, slightly pointed ears. Female has 8 teats and rear-opening pouch.
Length: HB 171–236 mm, T 60–102 mm.
Weight: 172–286 g.
Status: Endangered.

Michael Morcombe

Eastern Barred Bandicoot *Perameles gunnii* (Gunn's pouched-badger)

Eastern Barred Bandicoots have a bounding gait and stand to sniff the air when alarmed. They are common in Tasmania, but on the mainland are restricted to a few colonies in western Victoria that are derived from captive-bred animals.

Habitat: Open grassland, grassy woodland, pastures, suburban gardens.
Behaviour: Terrestrial, territorial, solitary, nocturnal. **Diet:** Insects, larvae, worms, bulbs,

tubers, fruit. **Breeding:** July to November, 1–2 litters per season. Females mature at 3 months; males at 4–5 months.
Lifespan: 2–3 years. **Features:** Greyish fawn fur with 3–4 pale bars on hindquarters. Belly is pale grey to white. Short, pointed tail is pale with a dark base. Slender snout and large, pointed ears.
Length: HB 270–350 mm, T 70–110 mm.
Weight: 500–1450 g.
Status: Endangered on mainland, vulnerable in Tas.

Long-nosed Bandicoot

Perameles nasuta (pouched-badger having a notable nose)

A remarkably long snout distinguishes this bandicoot from other east coast species. Suburban gardeners may be familiar with its cone-shaped excavations and shrill squeaks.

Habitat: Rainforest, eucalypt forest, woodland, grassland, suburban gardens.
Behaviour: Terrestrial, territorial, solitary, nocturnal. **Diet:** Insects, larvae, plant roots and tubers. **Breeding:** All year. More than 1 litter per season. Females mature at 5 months.

Lifespan: Up to 3 years. **Features:** Greyish brown fur with darker flecks, creamy white below. Some have bands on rump. Front paws and upper surface of hind feet are creamy white. Long, slender snout and long, pointed ears. Female has 8 teats and rear-opening pouch.
Length: HB 310–425 mm, T 120–155 mm.
Weight: 850–1100 g.
Status: Secure.

Rufous Spiny Bandicoot *Echymipera rufescens* (reddish pouched-hedgehog)

This rainforest-dwelling bandicoot is the only member of its family to live in Australia. It was discovered near the upper Nesbit River on Cape York Peninsula, Queensland, in 1932.

Habitat: Rainforest, open forest, grassy woodland, coastal heath. **Behaviour:** Terrestrial, nocturnal. **Diet:** Insects, fungi, fruit, bulbs.
Breeding: Summer.
Features: White flecks on blackish head and rufous body, pale underneath. Broad, stiff guard hairs. White front feet. Tapered, cylindrical head. Short, furless tail. Only 4 pairs of upper incisors. Female has 8 teats and rear-opening pouch.
Length: HB 300–400 mm, T 75–100 mm.
Weight: ♂ 500–2000 g; ♀ 500–1400 g.
Status: Secure.

Ian Morris

Bilby *Macrotis lagotis* (hare-eared long-ear)

This aridland marsupial lives in the Tanami, Gibson and Great Sandy Deserts and in south-west Queensland. It is the only bandicoot that burrows underground, digging tunnels three metres long and up to two metres deep.

Habitat: Arid tussock grasslands and Mitchell grass plains, mulga scrub. **Behaviour:** Terrestrial, nocturnal. **Diet:** Insects, fungi, seeds, bulbs, fruit. **Breeding:** All year. Usually 2 young per litter. **Lifespan:** About 3 years. **Features:** Soft, silky fur is bluish grey on the head and back, tinged with fawn on flanks, and pale on belly. Crested tail black with white tip. Long, slender snout and very large ears. Hind foot lacks first toe. Female has 8 teats and rear-opening pouch.
Length: ♂ HB 300–550 mm, T 200–290 mm; ♀ HB 290–390 mm, T 200–278 mm.
Weight: ♂ 1000 g–2500 g; ♀ 800–1100 g.
Status: Vulnerable.

Herbivorous Marsupials

The order **Diprotodontia** encompasses a wide
variety of marsupials. They are sometimes referred
to as herbivorous marsupials in comparison with the
carnivorous dasyurids and the omnivorous bandicoots.
However, there are several species that feed on insects as
well as plants. Members of this group have only one pair of
lower incisors and no lower canines. The second and third
toes on the hind feet are small and joined together except for
the claws.

Diprotodonts are divided into suborders. Wombats and the Koala are
classified as **Vombatiformes** and their common characteristics include
cheek pouches, a short, flap-like tail and the females having permanent,
rear-opening pouches. Possums and macropods, with their long tails and
permanent forward-opening pouches, belong to the suborder **Phalangerida**.

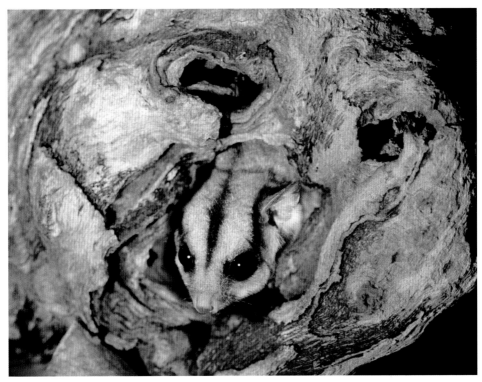

Above: Arboreal mammals such as the Squirrel Glider rely on old-growth forests for nest hollows.
Opposite: The Southern Hairy-nosed Wombat is one of three wombat species found in Australia.

Diet and Digestion

Koalas are one of the few mammals able to eat eucalypt leaves, which are tough, toxic and low in nutrition. But not just any eucalypt will do. A Koala's discerning nose picks out those species for which it has developed a chemical tolerance.

Eating takes up many of a Koala's waking hours. Leaves are sniffed carefully before one is selected and placed in the mouth to be ground up and swallowed. Toxic substances are removed in the stomach and filtered out by the liver. Bacterial fermentation in the Koala's two metre-long caecum completes the process of changing a mass of fibres into digestible nutrients.

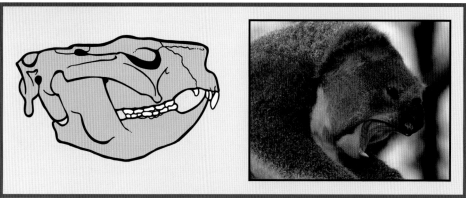

✗ The Koala's caecum is similar to the human appendix.

✗ A Koala must eat more than a kilogram of leaves a day to meet its energy needs.

✗ A eucalypt leaf may contain 50% water, 18% fibre, 13% tannins, 8% fat, 5% carbohydrates, 4% protein and 2% minerals.

Koalas develop a tolerance for the toxic chemicals found in eucalypt leaves.

Mating and Raising Young

Much of the male Koala's aggressive behaviour is related to breeding. A mature male establishes a home range encompassing those of several females and younger males. He proclaims his hierarchical dominance with bellowing calls, and marks the ground and tree trunks in his territory with urine and secretions from a chest gland. Rivals may challenge him vocally and physically.

Males will pursue females on and above the ground, and mothers with piggybacking young vigorously fend off unwanted advances. Thirty-five days after a treetop mating session, a female gives birth to one joey. It struggles into her rear-opening pouch and attaches to one of two teats. At five months the joey begins making forays into the outside world. During this time the mother produces a greenish faecal pap that inoculates the baby with the bacteria necessary for a gum-leaf diet.

When the joey leaves the pouch at seven months, it clings to its mother's back and sleeps curled in her lap. This is a dangerous time for a young Koala. It risks being taken by a bird of prey or python as it learns to climb and forage. And if it loses its grip and falls to the ground, the mother may not retrieve it.

The transition from milk-fed baby to self-fed juvenile is completed by 12 months. Young females usually remain in the area where they were born, while the males set out to find their own home ranges at two to three years of age.

From the time she is 2 years old, a female Koala usually gives birth to one young a year.

✘ Koalas have been seen feeding in 120 kinds of eucalypt trees. Favourites include Manna Gum, Swamp Gum, Blue Gum, Forest Red Gum and Grey Gum.

✘ Koalas get water from their food and seldom need to drink.

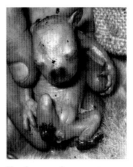

Koala pouch young, blind and hairless.

✘ Females begin breeding around 2 years of age; young males cannot mate until they establish a territory.

✘ A newborn Koala weighs 0.5 g and is less than 2 cm long.

✘ A Koala's eyes open at 22 weeks and its incisor teeth emerge at 24 weeks.

✘ If a mother does not retrieve a lost joey, it may be adopted by another female.

What's the Difference?

Male vs Female

The male Koala is taller, up to 50% heavier and has a larger, broader head and bigger nose than the female. Only the male has a sternal (chest) gland for scent-marking. The female has a rounder forehead and proportionally larger ears. Her nose and chin are smaller and more pointed.

North vs South

Koalas that live in cooler, southern regions are 25 to 30% heavier than those living in the north. Their coats are shaggier and fur around the face and ears is thicker, providing more warmth than the shorter fur of northern Koalas does.

Koala pelts were prized by fur traders.

The Koala as a Commodity

The Koala features in a number of Aboriginal Dreaming stories and has various local names including *cullawine, karbor, koolah, colo, boorabee* and *burrenbong*. For some Aborigines, the Koala had cultural or mythical significance and for others it was a valued source of meat and pelts. It was easy game and at times became scarce around larger Aboriginal settlements.

During the late 1800s, Koalas became an Australian export commodity. Since shooting spoiled the fur, the animals were trapped, clubbed or poisoned with cyanide. By 1894, up to 30,000 skins were being exported annually to England with a record 300,000 in 1889. While State governments belatedly introduced laws to protect decimated Koala populations, the little Aussie battler was still at risk from official open seasons. One million skins were taken in the 1919 Queensland season and, in 1927, more than 580,000 pelts were exported, mostly to the USA. Hunting continued even though Koala numbers were too low to maintain a viable industry. Public outrage and a ban on imports by USA Secretary of Commerce, later President, Herbert Hoover finally ended the Koala fur trade in the late '20s.

Finding Koalas

During the day look up into forked trees for sleeping Koalas. Check smooth tree trunks for pock marks and short, parallel gouges. Look on the ground for walking or bounding tracks with wide-soled, five-digit prints. Look around the base of trees for brown or reddish brown droppings that are hard, ridged and cylindrical. Green-tinged droppings may be found during the breeding season. Track Koalas at night by their loud bellows, snore-like grunts, wails and screams.

Location Tips

→ Kangaroo Island, SA
→ Grampians NP, Vic
→ Brisbane Forest Park, Qld
→ Myall Lakes NP, NSW

front foot and print

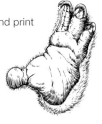

hind foot and print

Koala *Phascolarctos cinereus* (ash-coloured pouched-bear)

The Koala is one of Australia's best-known marsupials, but it is often overlooked in the wild because of its behaviour and colouration.

Habitat: Tropical to temperate eucalypt forest and woodland.
Behaviour: Mostly arboreal, solitary, mostly nocturnal.
Diet: Eucalypt leaves. **Breeding:** September to February. Females breed at 2 years; males usually at 3–4 years. **Lifespan:** Up to 18 years for females and several years less for males.
Features: Woolly fur light to dark grey with brown and white patches; cream belly. Broad head with small eyes, large furry ears and rectangular naked nose. Tail not visible. 5 toes on each foot; front foot has 2 opposable digits; hind foot has clawless opposable first toe and fused second and third toes. Female has 2 teats. Male has scent gland in pale fur on chest.
Length: ♂ north HB 674–736 mm, south 750–820 mm; ♀ north HB 648–723 mm, south 680–730 mm.
Weight: ♂ north 4.2–9.1 kg, south 9.5–14.9 kg; ♀ north 4.1–7.3 kg, south 7–11 kg.
Status: Secure.

Wombats

The shambling, muddle-headed wombat of storybook fame is a creature of fiction. People who have spent time with them describe wombats as playful and quick to learn. They have the most well-developed brain of any marsupial. Since wombats avoid people and are mainly nocturnal, their intelligence is not generally appreciated.

Common Wombat
Vombatus ursinus

✗ A wombat's teeth have no roots and continue growing throughout its life.

✗ The oldest wombat on record was 26 years and 22 days old when it died at London Zoo in 1906.

Diet and Digestion

Wombats leave their burrows at dusk to search for food. They graze on native grasses, sedges and rushes, and will gnaw on the roots of trees and shrubs. Wombats are equipped with one pair of upper and one pair of lower incisors and five pairs of flat grinding molars. A unique stomach gland helps them cope with a diet high in fibre but low in nutrients.

A wombat's home range can vary from five to 23 hectares depending on the availability of food. It will travel up to four kilometres during its nocturnal wanderings and visit between one and four burrows. A wombat is very territorial when it comes to food. It uses scent posts and prominently displayed droppings to mark its feeding area. It warns off interlopers with an aggressive display of head shaking, gnashing teeth and guttural growls.

Wombats are built for burrowing. Even compacted earth is no match for their powerful limbs (Southern Hairy-nosed Wombat).

Mating and Raising Young

Female wombats build separate nursery burrows in which to give birth and raise their young. Between 20 and 30 days after mating, a female gives birth to a bean-sized baby weighing one gram. The blind and furless young uses its front legs to pull itself into its mother's backward-facing pouch. It remains attached to one of two nipples until it weighs about three kilograms. The joey learns to forage and burrow at its mother's heels as it is being weaned.

If a colony's home range cannot support another adult, the young wombat is forced to move.

Juvenile
Common Wombat

The female Common Wombat's backward-facing pouch keeps dirt away from the joey when the mother is burrowing.

✗ When wombats are resting in their burrows, their metabolism slows to two-thirds its normal rate to conserve energy and water.

✗ Wombats living in the Australian Alps have to dig through snow to find food in winter.

A young joey will stay by its mother for 5 to 10 months, learning the skills it will need to survive (Common Wombat).

The Common Wombat's colour varies from black through to light grey.

✘ The range of the critically endangered Northern Hairy-nosed Wombat is only 300 ha.

✘ Some scientists estimate giant wombats from the Pleistocene era weighed nearly 3 t.

✘ A predator following a wombat into a burrow may be crushed against the walls or roof by the wombat's rump.

✘ A wombat will abandon its burrow if a snake moves in.

The Biggest Burrower

The wombat is the largest burrowing herbivorous mammal in the world. A stout body, blunt head and broad paws with strong claws make it a powerful earth-mover. An industrious wombat can excavate up to two metres of burrow a night. It loosens the soil with its forepaws and uses all four limbs to push it backwards. It lies on its side to scratch out the walls and roof making a tunnel about 50 centimetres high and 50 centimetres wide.

Burrows provide wombats with protection from predators, the weather and bushfires. A major burrow may be 30 metres long and form part of a network with several entrances. It usually takes more than one generation of wombats to create a large warren.

This plant-eating marsupial spends about two-thirds of its life underground carrying out regular tunnel maintenance and resting in leaf-lined sleeping chambers. A burrow sometimes has a vestibule just inside the entrance from which the wombat can observe outdoor conditions before emerging to forage at night or on overcast days.

Southern Hairy-nosed Wombats construct complex burrow systems and a large warren may house between 5 and 10 wombats.

Threats to Survival

Dingos, foxes and domestic dogs prey on wombats, but humans are the biggest threat to their survival. Land clearance for grazing and agriculture has reduced the range of suitable wombat habitats, while cattle and sheep compete with them for food.

Since the 1860s many landholders have regarded wombats as vermin. Their burrows can undermine buildings and be a hazard to machinery. They also breach fences, allowing Dingos to prey on stock, and kangaroos to graze on sown pastures.

Between 1955 and 1965, the Victorian government paid bounties on 63,000 wombat scalps. Wombats are now protected species in all States, except for parts of eastern Victoria.

The Southern Hairy-nosed Wombat was once common, but its home ranges are now sparsely scattered in semi-arid and arid regions in south-west New South Wales, South Australia and south-east Western Australia. Habitat degradation and competition from feral herbivores are threats to its survival.

Southern Hairy-nosed Wombat

Although a wombat has a waddling walking gait because of its short legs and large feet, it may run at speeds of up to 40 km/h for a short distance.

Finding Wombats

Look along dry watercourses, gullies and on sloping hills above creeks on cloudless evenings. Try overcast winter days in the snow country. A cluster of entrance holes fronted by piles of rubble is the most obvious sign. Wombats have large flat feet and a pigeon-toed gait, and leave distinctive tracks. Look for large cube-shaped droppings on prominent logs and rocks. Wombats often leave hair on smoothly polished rubbing posts, such as tree trunks, logs and stumps.

Location Tips

→ Kosciuszko NP, NSW
→ Wilsons Promontory NP, Vic
→ Messent CP, SA
→ Cradle Mountain–Lake St Clair NP, Tas
→ Nullarbor Plain, SA & WA

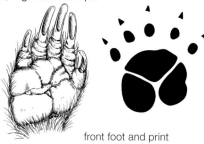

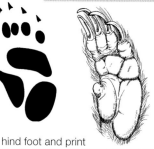

front foot and print   hind foot and print

Common Wombat *Vombatus ursinus* (bear-like wombat)

Common Wombats prefer to feed in open grassy areas at night. In winter and in alpine habitats they can be found basking or foraging during the day.

Habitat: Eucalypt forest, open woodland, coastal scrub and heath. **Behaviour:** Terrestrial, gregarious but feeds alone, nocturnal in summer. **Diet:** Native grasses, sedges, rushes, shrub

and tree roots. **Breeding:** All year. Mature at 2 years. 1 young per season. **Lifespan:** Up to 15 years. **Features:** Coarse, thick fur can be cream, brown or black. Large head has short, rounded ears and a naked nose. Hind foot has clawless opposable inner toe. Female has 2 teats and a rear-opening pouch. **Length:** HB 900–1150 mm, T 25 mm. **Weight:** 22–39 kg. **Status:** Secure.

Northern Hairy-nosed Wombat *Lasiorhinus krefftii* (Krefft's hairy-nose)

Epping Forest National Park in central Queensland is home to the only surviving colony of Northern Hairy-nosed Wombats. The population, which varies between 80 and 100, is protected by a Dingo-proof fence; however, its sustainability is threatened by inbreeding, drought, fire and the spread of unpalatable buffel grass.

Habitat: Semi-arid open woodland. **Behaviour:** Terrestrial, share burrows, feed alone, nocturnal. **Diet:** Native grasses. **Breeding:** November to April. Females breed twice every three years. **Features:** Long, silky fur is mainly grey-brown or grey mottled with fawn or black. Relatively long, pointed ears with tufts of white hairs along edges. Broad, square muzzle covered with short brown hair. May have dark patches around eyes. Female has 2 teats and a rear-opening pouch.

Length: ♂ HB 971–1069 mm, T 50 mm; ♀ HB 1034–1106 mm, T 50 mm. **Weight:** ♂ 26.9–33.3 kg; ♀ 29.9–35.1 kg.
Status: Endangered.

Southern Hairy-nosed Wombat *Lasiorhinus latifrons* (broad-headed hairy-nose)

Colonies of Southern Hairy-nosed Wombats are found mostly on the semi-arid sandy plains of Australia's southern central coastal region where annual rainfall is 200–500 mm.

Habitat: Eucalypt and acacia woodland, shrubland, heath. **Behaviour:** Terrestrial, feed alone, share burrows, nocturnal.
Diet: Prefer young shoots of native grasses.
Breeding: Late August through November; do not breed during drought. Mature at 3 years.
Features: Silky fur varies from reddish brown to grey. Short face with pointed ears. Can have white hair on nose. Female has 2 teats and a rear-opening pouch.
Length: HB 772–934 mm, T 25–60 mm.
Weight: 19–32 kg.
Status: Secure in restricted area.

Green Ringtail Possum
Pseudochirops archeri

✗ Urban-dwelling Common Brushtail Possums use roof cavities for dens.

✗ Sugar Gliders live in groups consisting of up to 7 adults and their offspring.

✗ Secretions from a male Common Brushtail's chest gland stain its fur red.

✗ A Common Ringtail Possum may have up to 8 nests in its home range.

✗ The Rufous Owl preys on ringtail possums in tropical rainforest.

✗ Rock Ringtail Possums form a guard around their young when moving between feeding sites.

Possums

Australia has 27 species of climbing marsupials commonly referred to as possums. They are grouped into 6 families within the suborder **Phalangerida**. While their bodies are as diverse as their lifestyles, all possums have a single pair of front lower incisors and the second and third toes on the hind foot are fused except for the claws. They also have long, flexible tails and the females have forward-opening pouches.

Habitat

Possums are found in forest, woodland and heath around Australia where rainfall is regular. Most arboreal species shelter in tree hollows, although some prefer to perch in clumps of leaves or even the roof cavities of buildings. The ground-dwellers make use of crevices in piles of boulders. Many possums line their shelters with shredded bark and other vegetation, making spherical nests.

Possums are quite possessive about their home areas. Some declare their feeding and breeding rights with raucous calls and physical aggression. Others mark their territories with secretions from chest, head or anal glands. Those that live in groups also mark each other, making it easier to identify and dispatch interlopers. Not having any scent glands, the sociable Leadbeater's Possum scents clan members with saliva.

Above: Rock Ringtail Possums mark their territories with strong smelling, rust-coloured secretions from chest and anal glands.
Opposite: A Mountain Brushtail Possum foraging at night.

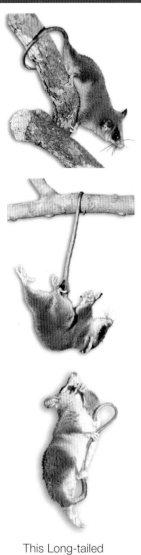

Behaviour

Possums are adept climbers with slender, jointed toes and sharp, curved claws. Their hind feet have opposable first toes that provide a pincer-like grip. Several species also have "thumbs" on their front feet that come in handy when climbing or holding food. Possums with prehensile tails have not only the additional security of a fifth limb, but also the means to carry nesting material.

Australia has six species of possums that volplane, or glide, from tree to tree. A flexible membrane, the patagium, extends between the front and back legs on each side of the body. Gliders can adjust the position of each membrane for stability and directional control while gliding.

Binocular vision, such as humans have, allows gliders to judge distances fairly accurately.

This Long-tailed Pygmy-possum scurried down the branch, missed its footing and swung from its tail, began to climb up its own tail, but then lost its grip.

 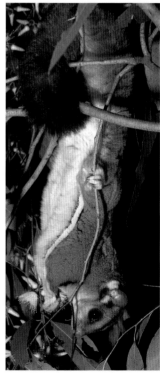

The Short-eared Brushtail Possum (left) and Squirrel Glider (right).

The larger, bushy-tailed gliders push off from a branch and stretch out their bodies to plane down towards the next tree. They finish with an upward swoop to land on all four feet.

The Greater Glider can make 90° turns in the air and glide up to 100 metres. They are often seen perched in the treetops preparing for takeoff when moderate winds and bright moonlight create optimum gliding conditions.

The Feathertail Glider is the world's smallest gliding mammal. It has relatively small membranes, but a flat tail edged with stiff bristles provides increased surface area and helps it steer and brake. It usually makes a direct approach, but can spiral around a tree trunk before landing.

The ability to glide gives possums greater access to scattered and seasonal food sources, as well as a means of escaping predators, such as pythons, quolls and cats.

A Herbert River Ringtail Possum.

Chris & Sandra Pollitt, ANTPhoto.com

A Squirrel Glider raises its paws in preparation for landing.

Eastern Pygmy-possum
Cercartetus nanus

✘ The Eastern Pygmy-possum feeds mostly on pollen and nectar from banksias, eucalypts and bottlebrushes.

✘ A Mountain Pygmy-possum's body temperature drops to 2°C during hibernation.

✘ Female pygmy-possums build spherical nests of shredded bark, leaves or grass.

✘ It can take 20 minutes for a torpid Little Pygmy-possum to become fully active.

✘ Pygmy-possums use several nests within their home range.

Pygmy-possums

Five species of pygmy-possums, belonging to the **Burramyidae** family, live in eastern and southern Australia in habitats ranging from rainforest to boulder-strewn alpine peaks.

They are usually found at night on or near the ground where they dart amongst the undergrowth in search of insects and flowers.

These small, nimble possums have sparsely furred, prehensile tails and padded feet with flexible toes. Most also have an opposable first toe on their hind foot. Three or four pairs of smoothly ridged molar teeth are more than adequate to deal with their omnivorous diet.

Pygmy-possums are fairly prolific breeders with some species producing three litters a year. A brief gestation period of about two weeks is followed by an average pouch life of 30 days. The young then continue development within the security of a nest, and, depending on the species, are weaned and independent at 45–90 days old. The female Western Pygmy-possum hurries things along by mating one or two days after giving birth. She gives birth a second time 50 days or more later when her first litter has been weaned.

During cold weather or food shortages pygmy-possums curl up, tuck in their ears and reduce their metabolic rate. This energy-saving torpor can last a few hours or several days. The alpine Mountain Pygmy-possum goes beyond the torpid state and actually hibernates for up to seven months of the year.

Tiny Eastern Pygmy-possums feeding on the pollen and nectar of a banksia.

Long-tailed Pygmy-possum
Cercartetus caudatus (notably-tailed *Cercartetus* [meaning "the tail I fasten to"])

This pygmy-possum is seldom seen because of its nocturnal habit. It has been found on the ranges and coastal plains between Townsville and Cooktown, and also lives in Papua New Guinea. These possums nest in logs, fern clumps and tree hollows. Females will stand over their young and hiss if disturbed.

Habitat: Rainforest, fringing forest of eucalypt, melaleuca and casuarina. **Behaviour:** Mainly arboreal, may share nests and feeding sites, nocturnal.
Diet: Nectar, insects. **Breeding:** 2 seasons: January and February, August through October. 1–4 young per litter. **Features:** Brownish grey above and pale grey below. Distinct black eye patches and thin, crinkly ears. Long, sparsely furred tail with thick base. Female has 4 teats.
Length: HB 103–108 mm, T 128–151 mm.
Weight: 25–40 g.
Status: Secure.

Mountain Pygmy-possum *Burramys parvus* (small stony-place mouse)

Four populations of Mountain Pygmy-possums have been discovered in the Australian Alps between Mt Bogong and Mt Kosciuszko since 1966. They nest on the ground among boulders and often travel over a kilometre in a night's foraging.

Habitat: Heath and shrubby woodland with boulder heaps, above 1,400 metres altitude.
Behaviour: Terrestrial, hibernates, nocturnal.
Diet: Insects and other arthropods, seeds, fruit. **Breeding:** October and November.

Usually 4 per litter. Mature by 1 year.
Lifespan: 2–5 years.
Features: Fine, thick fur, grey-brown above, may be darker from top of head to middle of back. Pale brown to cream below. Dark ring around eye. Tail long, thin and scaly. Female has 4 teats. **Length:** ♂ HB 110 mm, T 138 mm; ♀ HB 111 mm, T 136 mm.

Weight: ♂ 30–54 g; ♀ 30–82 g.
Status: Endangered.

Western Pygmy-possum
Cercartetus concinnus (neat *Cercartetus*)

The Western Pygmy-possum feeds in low shrubs and on the ground. It shelters during the day in tree hollows and the crowns of grass-trees. They are prolific breeders, which helps keep populations from being decimated by cats.

Habitat: Heath, dry eucalypt forest and woodland with shrubby undergrowth.
Behaviour: Mainly arboreal, solitary, nocturnal.
Diet: Insects, nectar.
Breeding: All year. 2 to 3 litters per year. Up to 6 young per litter.
Features: Fawn or reddish brown above, white below. Tapered tail has fine scales with some fur on the tip. Short claws on toes of front foot. Opposable first toe on hind foot. Female has 6 teats.

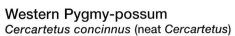

Length: HB 71–106 mm, T 71–96 mm.
Weight: 8–20 g.
Status: Secure.

Jiri Lochman, Lochman Transparencies

Little Pygmy-possum
Cercartetus lepidus (scaly[-tailed] *Cercartetus*)

Australia's smallest possum weighs in at an average of 7 g. It was thought to exist only in Tasmania, where it occupies most habitats except rainforest, but has since been found in north-west Victoria, south-east South Australia and on Kangaroo Island, South Australia.

Habitat: Wet and dry eucalypt forest, mallee woodland. **Behaviour:** Nests and feeds on or above ground, nocturnal. During winter, becomes torpid. **Diet:** Insects and other arthropods, small lizards. **Breeding:** September through January. Usually 4 per litter. **Features:** Soft, thick fur is pale fawn above, grey below. Large ears. Furred, prehensile tail tapers from thick base. Has a fourth pair of upper and lower molars. Female has 4 teats. **Length:** HB 50–65 mm, T 60–75 mm. **Weight:** 6–9 g. **Status:** Secure.

Dave Watts, Lochman Transparencies

Eastern Pygmy-possum *Cercartetus nanus* (dwarf *Cercartetus*)

This little possum extracts nectar and pollen with the help of a brush-tipped tongue. Nesting females are sometimes found in tree hollows, under loose bark and in abandoned bird nests.

Habitat: Rainforest, eucalypt forest, heath. **Behaviour:** Arboreal, mostly solitary, nocturnal. During winter, becomes torpid. **Diet:** Nectar, pollen, fruit, insects. **Breeding:** Late spring to early autumn on mainland. Late winter to early spring in Tasmania. 2 litters of 4 young per season. Mature at 5 months. **Lifespan:** 4 years. **Features:** Soft, dense fur is fawn-grey to olive-brown above, light grey to white below. Large round ears. Sparse-haired tail with fat base tapering to point. Female has 4 teats. **Length:** HB 70–110 mm, T 75–105 mm. **Weight:** 15–43 g. **Status:** Secure.

Yellow-bellied Glider
Petaurus australis

✘ A female Mahogany Glider may use up to 10 nests within a 20 ha home range.

✘ The Yellow-bellied Glider's home range is about 35 ha and it may travel 4 km a night foraging.

✘ Leadbeater's Possums build communal nests of shredded bark in tree hollows 6–30 m above the ground.

✘ The Striped Possum sometimes sleeps in clumps of epiphytic ferns.

✘ Squirrel Gliders and Sugar Gliders have interbred in captivity, producing fertile offspring.

Wrist-winged Gliders, Striped Possum and Leadbeater's Possum

There are six species of possums in Australia that belong to the **Petauridae** family. They all have long, chisel-like lower incisors. Other characteristic features include a dark stripe that runs from the forehead along the back, and a long, thickly furred prehensile tail. The four gliding species have membranes that extend from the fifth toe on the front foot to the first toe on the hind foot.

Most of these possums live in groups of three to 10 and scent marking is used to identify one another. The male Striped Possum and Mahogany Glider prefer a solitary existence except in the breeding season. They all use tree hollows for shelter.

Petaurid possums give birth to one or two young and species with extended breeding seasons may produce two litters a year. The young spend two and a half to three months in the pouch and then another two to three months as nestlings. They often cling to their mother's back while learning to forage.

As a family, these possums are known for their vocal repertoire, which includes gurgles, snorts, hisses, shrill yaps and territorial shrieks and screams.

The Sugar Glider is the commonest of the wrist-winged gliders, possibly because its diet is so varied.

Striped Possum
Dactylopsila trivirgata (three-striped naked-finger)

The Striped Possum is noisy, smelly and erratic. It races, leaps, crashes and snorts its way through the rainforest canopy looking for food or chasing rivals. The sharp claw on the long fourth toe extracts wood-boring insect larvae.

Habitat: Rainforest and adjacent eucalypt forest and woodland. **Behaviour:** Mainly arboreal, solitary, nocturnal. **Diet:** Insects, small vertebrates, leaves, fruit. **Breeding:** May occur from February to August. **Features:** Variable pattern of black and white stripes with white, Y-shaped marking on forehead. Single black stripe on each leg. Belly white. Tail-tip often white. Rounded ears. Toes lightly furred. Elongated fourth toe on front foot. Female has 2 teats. Dull red eyeshine.
Length: HB 256–270 mm, T 310–340 mm.
Weight: 246–528 g. **Status:** Secure.

Leadbeater's Possum *Gymnobelideus leadbeateri* (Leadbeater's naked glider)

This possum was presumed extinct until it was rediscovered in 1961. It is found only in Victoria's highland Mountain Ash forest. Groups of up to 8 live in communal nests lined with shredded bark in tree hollows. Colonies defend their home nests against intruders. They are nimble climbers, making leaps of up to 2 m.

Habitat: Highland eucalypt forest with acacia understorey. **Behaviour:** Arboreal, gregarious, nocturnal. **Diet:** Insects and other arthropods, plant sap and wattle gum. **Breeding:** Spring and autumn. 1–2 young per litter.
Features: Similar to Sugar Glider but without gliding membranes. Soft fur is grey to greyish brown above with dark stripe from crown to rump, pale below. Club-shaped tail. Large, thin, ears have white base. Ridged foot pads, retractable claws and one opposable toe on front foot. Female has 4 teats.
Length: HB 150–170 mm, T 145–180 mm.
Weight: 100–166 g. **Status:** Endangered.

Yellow-bellied Glider
Petaurus australis (southern rope-dancer)

This noisy and gregarious glider chews V-shaped notches in eucalypt trees to get at the sap. It can run along the underside of branches and glide up to 150 metres. It lives in small groups dominated by an adult male that scent-marks his den mates.

Habitat: Eucalypt forest. **Behaviour:** Arboreal, territorial, gregarious, nocturnal. **Diet:** Eucalypt sap, pollen, nectar, insects. **Breeding:** August to September in the south; May to September in the north. 1 young per season.
Features: Dark to pale grey above with dark stripe on forehead and thighs. White, cream or yellow below. Black paws with white claws. Gliding membranes extend from wrists to ankles.

Large, bare ears. Long, thick, bushy tail. Female has 2 teats and pouch is divided into two compartments. **Length:** HB 270–300 mm, T 420–480 mm. **Weight:** 450–700 g.
Status: Vulnerable in tropics.

Sugar Glider *Petaurus breviceps* (short-headed rope-dancer)

These small gliders live in groups of up to 10. If an adult male dies, an outsider is recruited to the clan. Sugar Gliders can volplane up to 50 metres.

Habitat: Rainforest, eucalypt forest and woodland with shrubby undergrowth.
Behaviour: Arboreal, territorial, gregarious, nocturnal. **Diet:** Wattle gum, eucalypt sap, pollen, nectar, insects. **Breeding:** June to July in south-east. All year in north, 2 litters per year. 1–2 young per litter. Females mature at 8–15 months, males at 12 months.

Lifespan: 4–5 years.
Features: Blue-grey to brown-grey, dark stripe from forehead to mid-back, cream to pale grey below. Dark patches at base of large, pointed ears. Tail grey to black, sometimes white tipped. Female has 4 teats. Dull mauve eyeshine.

Length: HB 160–210 mm, T 165–210 mm. **Weight:** ♂ 115–160 g; ♀ 95–135 g.
Status: Secure.

Mahogany Glider *Petaurus gracilis* (slender rope-dancer)

It wasn't until 1986 that this silent and elusive glider was rediscovered by science and recognised as a different species from the Squirrel Glider. The Mahogany Glider has a longer body and tail and distinct differences in skull structure. Its average glide is 30 metres.

Habitat: Medium to low woodland between Ingham and Tully, including coastal paperbark swamps and grass-tree woodland. **Behaviour:** Arboreal, mostly solitary, nocturnal.
Diet: Nectar, sap and gum from eucalypts, acacias and grass-trees, acacia seeds, insects.

Breeding: Births occur between April and October.
1 litter per season. 1–2 young per litter.
Lifespan: About 5 years.
Features: Varies from mahogany brown to predominantly grey above, buff to apricot belly. Dark stripe from forehead along back. Dark tail-tip. Female has 4 teats. **Length:** ♂ HB 247–265 mm, T 335–380 mm; ♀ HB 215–261 mm, T 300–390 mm.
Weight: ♂ 330–410 g; ♀ 255–407 g.
Status: Endangered.

Bruce Cowell, Queensland Museum

Squirrel Glider *Petaurus norfolcensis* (Norfolk rope-dancer)

The Squirrel Glider is similar in appearance and behaviour to its smaller relative, the Sugar Glider. While they coexist in some habitats, the Squirrel Glider generally occurs in drier forest and woodland. It lives in family groups of up to 10 in home ranges of 20–30 hectares. In spite of its scientific name, it does not occur on Norfolk Island.

Habitat: Dry eucalypt forest and woodland, coastal forest and wet eucalypt forest in north.
Behaviour: Arboreal, gregarious, nocturnal.
Diet: Insects, wattle gum and seeds, eucalypt sap, nectar, pollen. **Breeding:** June to December. 2 per litter. Mature by 12 months.
Features: Similar coloration to Sugar Glider. Belly fur is cream or white. Tail is bushier and never white-tipped. Snout is longer and more pointed. Ears are larger and narrower. Molar teeth are larger. Female has 4 teats.
Length: HB 180–230 mm, T 220–300 mm.
Weight: 190–300 g.
Status: Vulnerable in south.

Herbert River
Ringtail Possum
*Pseudochirulus
herbertensis*

✘ The prehensile tail of the Rock Ringtail Possum cannot support the possum's full body weight.

✘ A Western Ringtail Possum weighs about 550 g when it is weaned by 7 months of age.

✘ Some tropical rainforest ringtails park their unweaned young on low branches while they forage.

✘ Fig leaves are the Green Possum's favourite food.

✘ The Common Ringtail Possum builds basketball-sized nests lined with shredded bark or grass.

✘ When separated from its mother, a young Lemuroid Ringtail Possum makes a squeaky, hissing sound.

The Greater Glider and Ringtail Possums

The Australian side of the **Pseudocheiridae** family is represented by the Greater Glider and seven species of ringtail possums. They are accomplished climbers having two opposable toes on each front foot and a slender prehensile tail. Unlike the wrist-winged gliders, the gliding membrane of the Greater Glider extends only to its elbow.

These leaf-eating possums have one pair of long, blade-like lower incisors and several pairs of ridged molars for chopping and grinding their fibrous food. They also have a specialised digestive system. Nutrients are released from the leaf fibres by fermentation in the large appendix-like caecum and then slowly absorbed in the extra-long intestine.

As a group, these possums display varying degrees of social behaviour. Some are solitary, meeting only to mate; others live in small family units. In between are the species where males and females feed and den together from courtship through to the weaning of their offspring. The Common Ringtail male is known to assist with the transport, grooming and defence of his unweaned nestlings.

Most of these possums are forest inhabitants that shelter and raise their young in tree hollows. The females give birth to one or two young per litter and, depending on the species, the young spend three to four months in the pouch. During the weaning, which takes two to four months, the young may be left in a nest or carried on the mother's back.

Above: The gap between the Common Ringtail's second and third fingers gives it a secure grip.
Opposite: A Green Ringtail Possum in characteristic curled-up pose.

Greater Glider *Petauroides volans* (flying vaulter)

This is Australia's largest gliding possum; individuals may weigh three times as much as the Yellow-bellied Glider – the next largest glider. It usually follows established gliding routes between feeding trees, making up to 100-metre glides with its forearms tucked beneath its chin.

Habitat: Eucalypt forest and woodland.
Behaviour: Mostly arboreal, solitary, nocturnal.
Diet: Eucalypt leaves. Normally does not need to drink.
Breeding: March to June. 1 young. Mature at 2 years.
Features: Colour varies from rich brown through grey to mottled cream. Belly is creamy white. Sometimes head and tail are pale. Large ears have furred fringe. Very long, furry tail is not prehensile. Gliding membranes extend between elbows and ankles. Female has 2 teats.
Length: HB 350–450 mm, T 450–600 mm.
Weight: 900–1700 g.
Status: Secure.

Lemuroid Ringtail Possum *Hemibelideus lemuroides* (lemur-like half-*Belideus*, *Belideus* being a synonym of *Petaurus*)

The Lemuroid Ringtail is an agile climber that spends most of its time in the rainforest canopy. It is the only ringtail to make freefall leaps of 2–3 m between branches.

Habitat: Highland tropical rainforest above 450 m. **Behaviour:** Arboreal, gregarious,

nocturnal. **Diet:** Leaves, flowers, fruit.
Breeding: August to November. 1 young.
Features: Soft, thick fur is chocolate brown and dark grey above, yellow tinged belly. Creamy white colour form found in 30% of population above 1100 m. Short face with light eye rings. Bare-tipped tail. Female has 2 teats. Bright green to gold eyeshine.
Length: ♂ HB 315–360 mm, T 320–365 mm; ♀ HB 313–400 mm, T 300–373 mm.
Weight: ♂ 810–1060 g; ♀ 750–1140 g.
Status: Secure.

Stan Breeden

Rock Ringtail Possum *Petropseudes dahli* (Dahl's rock-*Pseudocheirus*)

Rock Ringtails live in small family groups and the male will defend its mate and young with much grunting and tail slapping. Unlike other ringtails, it is not known to build a nest and, during the day, rests on rock ledges and shelters in rock crevices, climbing among trees and shrubs to feed at night.

Habitat: Rocky outcrops with deep crevices and boulders in eucalypt woodland and vine forest. **Behaviour:** Semi-terrestrial, territorial, gregarious, nocturnal. **Diet:** Leaves, flowers, fruit. **Breeding:** 2 seasons per year. 1 young per season. **Features:** Thick, woolly fur is grey to red-tinged brownish grey, dark stripe from forehead to rump. White belly. White around eyes and under ears. Pointed snout and small round ears. Short tail tapers to almost naked tip, most of underside is bare. Female has 2 teats. **Length:** ♂ HB 334–375 mm, T 200–220 mm; ♀ HB 349–383 mm, T 207–266 mm. **Weight:** 1280–2000 g. **Status:** Secure.

Ian Morris

Green Ringtail Possum *Pseudochirops archeri* (Archer's *Pseudocheirus*-like animal)

This possum's camouflage-green coat is actually a combination of black, white and yellow hairs. Instead of using a nest or den, the Green Ringtail finds a suitable branch and curls into a ball to sleep. Its young ride on the female's back after emerging from the pouch possibly for the longest time of all ringtails.

Habitat: Highland tropical rainforest above 300 m. **Behaviour:** Mostly arboreal, solitary, nocturnal. **Diet:** Leaves, figs. **Breeding:** August to November. 1 young. **Features:** Thick, soft fur is greyish green to lime-green with two silvery stripes along back from shoulder to rump. White belly. Pointed snout, pink nose, small rounded ears. White around eyes and ears. Relatively short tail has thick base. Female has 2 teats. Dull yellow-red eyeshine. **Length:** ♂ HB 344–371 mm, T 309–372 mm; ♀ HB 285–377 mm, T 315–333 mm. **Weight:** ♂ 880–1190 g; ♀ 670–1350 g. **Status:** Secure.

Daintree River Ringtail Possum
Pseudochirulus cinereus
(ash-coloured little-*Pseudocheirus*)

The Daintree River and Herbert River Ringtails were thought to be the same species until 1989. Having 16 pairs of chromosomes compared to the Herbert River's 12 pairs was enough to see it classified as a separate species.

Habitat: Highland tropical rainforest above 450 m.
Behaviour: Mostly arboreal, solitary, nocturnal.
Diet: Leaves, figs. **Breeding:** April to May peak. 2 young.
Features: Pale caramel to brown above grading to creamy white belly. Dark stripe from forehead to lower back. Tail has naked pink skin on underside and usually has white tip. Female has 2 teats.

Length: ♂ HB 346–360 mm, T 320–395 mm; ♀ HB 335–368 mm, T 325–362 mm.
Weight: ♂ 830–1450 g; ♀ 700–1200 g.
Status: Secure.

Herbert River Ringtail Possum
Pseudochirulus herbertensis (little-*Pseudocheirus* from Herbert region)

Herbert River Ringtails are cautious climbers and rarely come down from the branches to the ground. They sleep in tree hollows and clumps of epiphytic ferns or sometimes build a nest in a forked branch.

Hans & Judy Beste

Habitat: Highland tropical rainforest and fringing eucalypt forest above 350 m. **Behaviour:** Arboreal, solitary, nocturnal. **Diet:** Leaves.
Breeding: April to May peak. 2 young.
Features: Adults dark brown to black above, varying amounts of white on chest, belly and fore limbs. Long, tapering tail usually white-tipped. Pointed snout, small ears and bulging reddish brown eyes with white rims. Juveniles same colour as Daintree River Ringtail. Female has 2 teats.
Pinkish orange eyeshine.
Length: ♂ HB 350–400 mm, T 290–470 mm; ♀ HB 301–376 mm, T 335–410 mm.
Weight: ♂ 810–1530 g; ♀ 800–1230 g.
Status: Secure.

Western Ringtail Possum
Pseudocheirus occidentalis (western false-hand)

Western Ringtails are most at risk from land clearance and predation by foxes. They have small home ranges and may use up to 8 sleeping sites in a year.

Habitat: Eucalypt forest with Peppermint Gum, Marri or Jarrah.
Behaviour: Mostly arboreal, solitary, nocturnal.
Diet: Leaves.
Breeding: All year with winter peak.
Usually 1 young. Females mature at 8 months.
Features: Dark brown or grey above, cream or grey belly. Slender, white-tipped tail. Medium-sized, rounded ears. Female has 2 teats.
Length: HB 300–400 mm,
T 300–400 mm.
Weight: 900–1100 g.
Status: Vulnerable.

Michael Morcombe

Common Ringtail Possum
Pseudocheirus peregrinus (wandering false-hand)

The Common Ringtail Possum of eastern Australia is probably a group of four subspecies. They have adapted well to urban life, using exotic flowers and fruit as alternative food sources.

Habitat: Rainforest, eucalypt forest, woodland, shrubland, suburban gardens. **Behaviour:** Mostly arboreal, gregarious, nocturnal. **Diet:** Leaves, flowers, fruit. **Breeding:** April to November. 2 young.
Features: Colour varies from reddish brown through grey to almost black above, paler below. Face, flanks and limbs may be red-tinged. Pale patches under ears. Long tail tapers to white tip with naked underside. Medium-sized, rounded ears. Female has 4 teats.
Length: HB 300–350 mm, T 300–350 mm.
Weight: 700–1100 g.
Status: Secure.

Common Spotted Cuscus
Spilocuscus maculatus (spotted spotted-cuscus)

The Spotted Cuscus has no fixed shelter. It rests on tree branches, sometimes making a temporary platform of leafy twigs. The males are aggressive and will attack each other.

Habitat: Tropical rainforest, mangroves, open eucalypt forest.
Behaviour: Mostly arboreal, solitary, mainly nocturnal.
Diet: Fruit, flowers, leaves, insects, small birds, bird eggs.
Breeding: Possibly all year. 1–2 young.
Lifespan: Up to 11 years. **Features:** Solidly built with dense, woolly fur, grey above and cream below. Males have pale spots on back and females sometimes have white rumps. Very small ears. Large red-rimmed eyes. Snout is sparsely furred showing yellowish pink skin. Large canine teeth. Two-thirds

of prehensile tail is naked. 2 opposable toes on front foot. Female has 4 teats.
Length: HB 348–580 mm, T 310–435 mm.
Weight: 1.5–4.9 kg. **Status:** Secure.

Short-eared Brushtail Possum
Trichosurus caninus (dog-like hairy-tail)

The Short-eared Brushtail is found on the Great Dividing Range from south-east Queensland to central New South Wales. Its southern relative, the Mountain Brushtail *T. cunninghamii* has longer ears and feet, and a shorter tail. Until recently, these were thought to be the same species.

Habitat: Subtropical rainforest, eucalypt forest.
Behaviour: Mainly arboreal, solitary, nocturnal.
Diet: Leaves, fruit, flowers, seeds, fungi, lichen, bark.
Breeding: March to May. 1 young. Females mature at 2 years.
Lifespan: Females up to 17 years, males up to 12 years.
Features: White-flecked dark grey to black above, whitish below. Short, round ears. Bushy tail has strip of naked skin on underside. 5 toes on front paws are evenly spread.
Length: HB 400–500 mm, T 340–420 mm.
Weight: 2.5–4.5 kg.
Status: Secure.

Common Brushtail Possum
Trichosurus vulpecula (little fox-like hairy-tail)

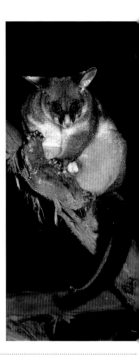

Australia's most familiar and widespread possum is actually a group of four subspecies that vary in colour and length of fur depending on their geographic location.

Habitats: Rainforest, eucalypt forest, woodland, urban areas.
Behaviour: Mostly arboreal, solitary, nocturnal. **Diet:** Leaves, flowers, fruit, seeds, insects, occasionally small birds, eggs.
Breeding: Autumn and spring; all year in northern regions. 1 young. Females mature at 1 year; males by 2 years. **Lifespan:** Average 6–7 years, up to 11 years. **Features:** Most commonly silver-grey above, off-white to cream below. Dark patches on snout. Light grey paws. Large, oval ears. Bushy tail has naked undersurface. 5 evenly spaced toes on front feet. Female has 2 teats. In the north-west, reddish grey short hair; in north Queensland, coppery short hair; in Tasmania, woolly fur may be blackish.
Length: HB 350–550 mm, T 250–400 mm.
Weight: ♂ 1.3–4.5 kg; ♀ 1.2–3.5 kg. **Status:** Secure.

Scaly-tailed Possum *Wyulda squamicaudata* (Aboriginal name + scale-tailed)

The unusual Scaly-tailed Possum is found in rugged sandstone country near the Kimberley coast. It shelters in rock piles and crevices, emerging after dusk to forage in trees.

Habitat: Eucalypt and monsoon forest in rocky country. **Behaviour:** Semi-terrestrial, solitary, nocturnal.
Diet: Flowers, fruit, leaves, possibly insects. **Breeding:** March to August. 1 young. Females mature at 2 years. **Features:** Pale grey tipped with black, cream below. Dark stripe from crown to rump. Base of tail is tinged red. Rest of tail covered with small knobby projections. Two opposable toes on front foot. **Length:** HB 310–395 mm, T 300 mm.
Weight: 1.35–2 kg.
Status: Secure.

Jiri Lochman, Lochman Transparencies

✘ A Honey Possum's tongue is 18 mm long.

✘ A newborn Honey Possum weighs about 5 mg.

✘ Like kangaroos, a female carries dormant embryos that resume development shortly before her first litter is weaned.

✘ Honey Possums may become torpid during cold weather or when food is scarce.

✘ Male Honey Possums have the longest sperm of any mammal.

Honey Possum

The unique Honey Possum of Australia's south-western heathland is the only member of the **Tarsipedidae** family.

This diminutive marsupial darts from blossom to blossom probing each with its slender snout to gather pollen and nectar on its brush-tipped tongue. A keen sense of smell and full-colour vision help it find suitable flowers.

The Honey Possum is one of the few arboreal mammals to climb without the aid of claws. Like primates such as the Tarsier, the broad-tipped toes of its front feet have short, flat nails instead of curved claws. It relies on flexible joints, rough toe pads and a long, prehensile tail for grip.

Honey Possums are social creatures that live in groups dominated by the largest females. They shelter in hollow trunks of grass-trees or abandoned bird nests. Mating occurs throughout the year, but most births occur from early autumn to spring. A female will mate with more than one male and offspring in the same litter can have different fathers.

The young spend about two months in the pouch and are weaned by five months of age.

Honey Possum *Tarsipes rostratus* (notably snouted Tarsier-foot)

The Honey Possum is found only in southern Western Australia. This nectarivorous nomad does not have a permanent home range, preferring to follow the seasonal flowering of heathland plants. In cold weather or when food is scarce, it may become torpid for up to 10 hours at a time, conserving energy.

Habitat: Coastal sandplain heaths. **Behaviour:** Arboreal, gregarious, mostly nocturnal. **Diet:** Nectar, pollen. **Breeding:** All year with seasonal peaks. 2–3 young. 1–2 litters per year. Mature at 6 months. **Lifespan:** 1–2 years.

Michael Morcombe

Features: Light brown or grey with three darker stripes along back, cream belly. Long pointed snout. Long, tapering tail is sparsely furred. Hind foot has clawless opposable first toe and fused grooming toes with claws. Broad-tipped toes on front foot are evenly spaced. Female has 4 teats and well-developed pouch.

Length: HB 40–94 mm, T 45–110 mm. **Weight:** 7–12 g. **Status:** Secure.

✘ Feathertail Gliders sometimes nest in electricity meter boxes and telephone junction covers.

✘ The Feathertail Glider is the smallest gliding mammal in the world.

✘ Special toe pads provide traction for Feathertail Gliders to climb a vertical pane of glass.

✘ The Feathertail Glider can glide more than 20 m.

✘ Huddling together and brief periods of torpor help Feathertail Gliders reduce their energy needs on cold days.

Feathertail Glider

The Feathertail Glider is the only member of the **Acrobatidae** family found in Australia. Its relatively small gliding membranes extend from the elbow to the knee on each side of the body. The distinctive feather-like tail provides extra surface area and assists with steering and braking.

These omnivores forage between ground level and the upper canopy, collecting nectar and pollen with a brush-tipped tongue and crunching insects between their ridged molars. They are fast, agile climbers with sharp claws and large serrated toe pads that provide grip even on smooth surfaces.

Feathertails feed and nest in loosely associated groups of up to 20. They may use one or more spherical nests, or dreys, that are constructed in any suitably enclosed space.

During their long breeding season, females often produce more than one litter of three to four young. The young emerge from the pouch after 65 days and are weaned at just over three months of age. High-pitched calls and scent marking help the mother and young recognise one another in the communal nest. Like the Honey Possum, female Feathertails mate within days of giving birth and delay development of the embryos until a few weeks before her first lot of young is weaned.

Feathertail Glider *Acrobates pygmaeus* (dwarf acrobat)

Common, but difficult to find because of their size, Feathertail Gliders may drop to the ground and freeze when frightened.

Habitat: Rainforest, eucalypt forest and woodland, parks and gardens. **Behaviour:** Arboreal, gregarious, nocturnal. **Diet:** Nectar, pollen, eucalypt sap, insects. **Breeding:** Late winter through summer; all year in northern regions. 3–4 young. 1–2 litters. **Lifespan:** About 3 years. **Features:** Grey-brown above and white to cream below. Fringe of stiff hairs on each side of prehensile tail. Gliding membrane extends between elbows and knees. Pointed snout and relatively large rounded ears. Striated toe pads. Clawless, opposable first toe on hind foot. Female has 4 teats. **Length:** HB 65–80 mm; T 70–80 mm. **Weight:** 10–14 g. **Status:** Secure.

Ian Morris

Above: Black Wallaroo

Macropods

There are three families of marsupials commonly referred to as macropods. The Musky Rat-kangaroo of the **Hypsiprymnodontidae** family, and the potoroos and bettongs of the **Potoroidae** family are small, omnivorous macropods. The **Macropodidae** family includes the more familiar herbivorous kangaroos and wallabies.

Fossil evidence suggests Australia's macropods evolved from possum-like animals. As they abandoned the treetops for the continent's expanding grassland habitats, most developed features more suited to open terrain.

While various models were being tried and tested on the evolutionary roadway, a body plan emerged that became standard equipment for a typical Australian macropod. It included short fore limbs, powerful hindquarters and long hind feet that gave these marsupials a distinctive upright stance and a two-footed hopping gait.

However, not all macropods developed the size or features needed for a life in the open. Several species still rely on densely vegetated habitats for food and shelter, and their compact bodies retain features more commonly found in modern day possums.

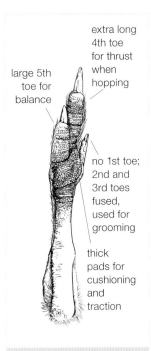

extra long 4th toe for thrust when hopping

large 5th toe for balance

no 1st toe; 2nd and 3rd toes fused, used for grooming

thick pads for cushioning and traction

Typical Macropod Foot

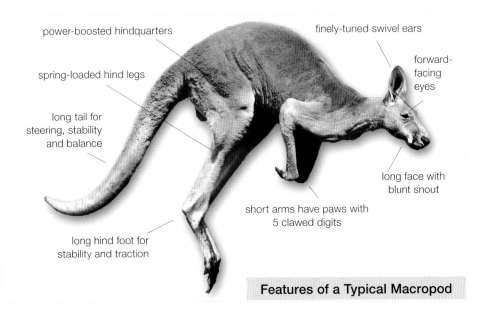

power-boosted hindquarters

finely-tuned swivel ears

spring-loaded hind legs

forward-facing eyes

long tail for steering, stability and balance

long hind foot for stability and traction

short arms have paws with 5 clawed digits

long face with blunt snout

Features of a Typical Macropod

Eastern Grey Kangaroo
Macropus giganteus

✗ A macropod's powerful leg muscles and stretchy tendons store and release energy as an elastic band does.

✗ When swimming, a macropod can kick its hind legs alternately.

✗ Tree-kangaroos and the Musky Rat-kangaroo have long fore limbs and can walk on all fours as well as hop.

✗ A female Eastern Grey Kangaroo holds the marsupial speed record of 64 km/h.

✗ The high jump record is held by a male Red Kangaroo that escaped hunters by leaping over a 3.1-m-high stack of timber.

✗ A Red Kangaroo can hop at 40 km/h for up to 2 km.

Macropods on the Move

Most macropods are unable to walk or run on all fours because their hind legs cannot move independently of each other and are much longer than the front limbs. While their "pentapedal" walk is ungainly, macropods are masters of the two-footed hop.

Hopping is a useful method of locomotion for animals that need to make quick getaways, especially in open country where there are few places to hide. It is an energy-efficient means of travel that uses less oxygen than running or galloping at speeds above 15 kilometres per hour. A hopping macropod also saves on the amount of energy it takes to breathe because air is forced in and out of its lungs as its gut flops up and down.

A kangaroo's muscular tail can support its whole body.

Pentapedal Walk

When a macropod is moving slowly, the front limbs and tail support the body as the hind legs swing forward simultaneously.

Bipedal Hop

When moving at speed, a macropod hops on its two hind legs. The tail acts as a counterbalance and the arms and head are usually positioned to streamline the fore body.

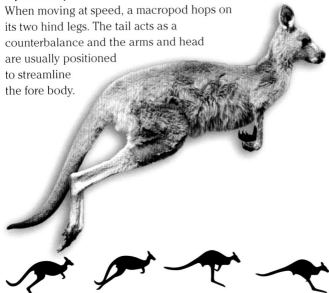

Keeping Cool

A macropod has a split upper lip that channels moisture from the nose into the mouth. To reduce heat stress and conserve body moisture a macropod:

✘ travels and feeds between dusk and dawn;

✘ rests in the shade during the day;

✘ scrapes away topsoil to lie on cooler ground;

✘ does not sweat;

✘ uses the roof of its mouth and long tongue as evaporative coolers;

✘ licks its chest and arms so the evaporating saliva cools its skin.

Food

Macropods are surprisingly diverse in their eating habits for a group of animals usually referred to as herbivores. Potoroos, bettongs and the Musky Rat-kangaroo depend as much on insects and fungi as they do on plants.

Of the species that are strictly vegetarian, some have a preference for browsing on shrubs and other leafy green plants, while others are predominantly grass grazers.

Regardless of what kinds of vegetation they prefer to eat, all macropods are well equipped to deal with a variety of high fibre, low nutrient plant foods.

A typical macropod has two chisel-like lower incisors that fit behind three pairs of upper incisors to create a nipping or shearing mechanism. A gap behind the front teeth allows the tongue to push wads of food back to the grinding molars. Once the food has been swallowed, micro-organisms in the fore stomach ferment the plant fibres into fatty acids that are absorbed by the rest of the digestive system.

Macropods, with the exception of the potoroids, have an unusual adaptation to cope with molars that are worn down by fibrous and abrasive native plants. The four molars on each side of the upper and lower jaws erupt in slow succession and move forward along the jaw as the animal gets older. When a molar at the head of the line wears down, it falls out and the one behind takes its place. A middle-aged macropod may have all 16 molars in use, but after a lifetime of chewing it may be left with only one or two molars in each jaw. The Nabarlek has the additional advantage of having a never-ending supply of moving molars.

In captivity, macropods will readily accept food not found in the wild.

A Red-Necked Wallaby displays its lower incisors.

The Long-nosed Potoroo enjoys a varied diet of roots, fungi and insects.

A Brush-tailed Bettong chewing a fibrous root.

Macropod Predators

Macropods, especially the young and the smaller species, are fair game for native carnivores, such as pythons, goannas, birds of prey, quolls and the Dingo. They are also preyed upon by introduced cats, dogs and foxes.

Keen senses, multi-directional ears and an upright stance are part of a macropod's inbuilt alert system that helps it pinpoint potential threats. Species that live in groups also warn one another of danger by thumping their hind feet, and maternal tutting and clicking help keep vulnerable joeys from straying too far.

While some species use cryptic coloration and behaviour to quietly disappear into their surroundings, a threatened macropod's usual response is to flee. But speed and agility are not always enough to save a macropod. It may escape a predator only to die of a stress-induced heart attack within a very short time.

Sometimes large male kangaroos will stand their ground and lash out with a disembowelling kick. They've also been seen trying to drown Dingos that have pursued them into waterholes and rivers.

Road death is a major mortality factor for macropods.

✘ A pack of 4 or 5 Dingos can run a kangaroo down or surround and overpower it.

✘ One Wedge-tailed Eagle will provide a distraction on the ground while another attacks from above.

A Wedge-tailed Eagle swoops in to attack a wallaroo.

✘ A newborn Eastern Grey Kangaroo weighs less than 1 g.

✘ A newborn Red Kangaroo takes about 3 minutes to crawl from its mother's cloaca into her pouch.

✘ Almost 50% of Red Kangaroos fail to reach 2 years of age; 90% die before the age of 10.

✘ A female macropod produces two kinds of milk to suit the different needs of a pouch joey and an unweaned young one at heel.

Mating and Raising Young

Most macropods have the remarkable ability to produce young only when conditions favour their survival.

The females are fertile throughout the year if food is plentiful, but do not come into breeding condition in times of drought. This is a great advantage to plant-eating animals whose food supply is often limited by irregular rainfall.

The females of most species can also control the rate at which their embryos develop. This phenomenon is called "embryonic diapause" and is particularly useful in harsh environments where infant mortality is high.

A female usually mates soon after giving birth; however, development of the fertilised egg is suspended while she is carrying a pouch joey. Development resumes if the joey dies, or a few weeks before it takes up life outside the pouch. The new baby is born after a normal gestation period and takes possession of the pouch.

If conditions are good and the mother mates again, she will have an unweaned joey at heel, a suckling joey in the pouch and an embryonic joey in waiting.

Jiri Lochman, Lochman Transparencies

Macropods have a forward-opening pouch with 4 teats. A newborn makes its way into the pouch and attaches itself to a teat. *Opposite:* An unweaned joey at heel.

Rufous Bettong
Aepyprymnus rufescens

Potoroos, Bettongs and Rat-kangaroo

Potoroos, bettongs and the Musky Rat-kangaroo are small macropods that combine the features of modern kangaroos with those of their long-extinct ancestors.

They prefer habitats with a thick understorey where food and shelter are plentiful. They are the only macropods to build nests, making good use of their weakly prehensile tails to carry nesting material.

These omnivores feed on plants, insects and fungi, most of which are obtained by digging through leaf litter and soil. To cope with this varied diet, their dental equipment includes upper canines and fixed molars, which the herbivorous macropods do not have.

They all have a typical macropod's long hind foot with its fused grooming toes. While potoroos and bettongs are speedy little hoppers, the Musky Rat-kangaroo lacks muscular hind legs so it walks and gallops with a quadrupedal gait. It does, however, have thumb-like first toes on its hind feet and ridged foot pads that help it climb sloping tree trunks.

✘ The Long-footed Potoroo eats 30 different kinds of fungi.

✘ The Long-nosed Potoroo lives up to 7 years in the wild.

✘ The Musky Rat-kangaroo is the only macropod to raise twin joeys.

✘ The Burrowing Bettong builds complex warrens with many entrances and connecting tunnels.

✘ Bettongs do not need to drink water.

✘ A Rufous Bettong may travel over 4 km a night when foraging.

Location Tips

→ Crater Lakes NP, Qld
→ Freycinet NP, Tas
→ Dryandra, WA

The Brush-tailed Bettong, or Woylie, feeds mostly on underground fungi, a diet that requires a specialised digestive system.

Long-footed Potoroo *Potorous longipes* (long-footed potoroo)

The Long-footed Potoroo was first recorded in 1980 in East Gippsland. It has since been found in the Victorian Alps and near Rockton, New South Wales. It usually nests in clumps of grass or ferns in the forest understorey.

Habitat: Temperate rainforest, wet eucalypt forest.
Behaviour: Terrestrial, solitary, nocturnal.
Diet: Fungi, plants, invertebrates.
Breeding: All year, raising 1 young at a time. Mature by 2 years.
Features: Grey-brown above; pale grey below. Sparsely furred tail. Hind foot longer than head. Female has 4 teats.
Length: HB 380–415 mm, T 315–325 mm.
Weight: ♂ 2–2.2 kg; ♀ 1.6–1.8 kg.
Status: Endangered.

Long-nosed Potoroo *Potorous tridactylus* (three-toed potoroo)

Long-nosed Potoroos in Tasmania have longer, narrower snouts than those living in Queensland, and are more likely to have white-tipped tails. This potoroo can be confused with the Southern Brown Bandicoot in places where their habitats overlap.

Habitat: Rainforest, eucalypt forest and coastal heath. **Behaviour:** Terrestrial, mainly solitary, nocturnal. **Diet:** Fungi, plant roots and tubers, invertebrates. **Breeding:** All year, but peaks in winter to early spring and in late summer; raises 1 young at a time. Mature at 1 year. **Lifespan:** Up to 7 years. **Features:** Rufous-brown to grey-brown above; paler below. Long, tapered snout has bare patch above nostrils. Tail is furred and sometimes white tipped. Hind foot is shorter than head. Female has 4 teats.
Length: ♂ HB 380 mm, T 204–262 mm; ♀ HB 340 mm, 198–254 mm.
Weight: ♂ 740–1640 g; ♀ 660–1350 g. **Status:** Vulnerable on mainland.

Rufous Bettong *Aepyprymnus rufescens* (reddish high-rump)

Of the bettongs, the Rufous Bettong is the only one still common on the mainland. It rests in a cone-shaped nest of dry grass and will hiss and stamp its feet when alarmed.

Habitat: Eucalypt forests and woodland with grassy understorey.
Behaviour: Terrestrial, gregarious, nocturnal.
Diet: Flowers, seeds, leaves, roots, tubers, fungi, animal bones. **Breeding:** All year; 1 young per mating. Females mature by 11 months, males by 13 months.
Features: Reddish brown to grey-brown fur flecked with light grey; belly is pale. Head has pointed ears and hairy muzzle.

Length: HB 375–390 mm, T 338–387 mm.
Weight: ♂ up to 3 kg; ♀ up to 3.5 kg.
Status: Secure.

Burrowing Bettong
Bettongia lesueur (Lesueur's bettong)

This is the only macropod to construct large, complex warrens that shelter dozens of individuals. It was found on the mainland until the 1940s but now exists on only four islands, Bernier, Dorre, Barrow and Boodie, off the WA central coast.

Habitat: Once widespread, except in dense vegetation or high rainfall areas.
Behaviour: Terrestrial, gregarious, nocturnal. **Diet:** Fungi, fruit, seeds, roots, insects.
Breeding: All year; 1 young per mating. Up to 3 young per year. Mature at 5 months.
Features: Yellow-grey above, light grey below. Short, rounded ears. Thick, sparsely furred tail. **Length:** HB 280–360 mm, T 215–300 mm.
Weight: About 1.5 kg.
Status: Vulnerable.

Brush-tailed Bettong *Bettongia penicillata* (brushed bettong)

The Brush-tailed Bettong, also known as the Woylie, builds domed nests of shredded bark or grass. Land clearance and predation by foxes restricted its distribution to south-west Western Australia, but it has been successfully reintroduced to areas of South Australia.

Habitat: Eucalypt forest and woodland with grassy or shrubby understorey.
Behaviour: Terrestrial, solitary, nocturnal.
Diet: Fungi, bulbs, tubers, seeds, insects, resin. **Breeding:** All year; 1 young per mating. Up to 3 young per year. Mature by 6 months.

Features: White-flecked fur is grey-brown to yellow-grey above, paler below. Black crest on tail. Blunt, naked nose. Medium-sized, slightly pointed ears. Female has 4 teats.
Length: HB 300–380 mm, T 290–360 mm.
Weight: 1.1–1.6 kg.
Status: Secure.

Musky Rat-kangaroo *Hypsiprymnodon moschatus* (musky Hypsiprymnus-tooth)

Australia's smallest macropod lives in coastal and highland rainforests between Ingham and Cooktown. It forages early in the morning and just before sunset. It uses several nests that may be hidden on the ground or in clumps of vines.

Habitat: Tropical rainforest. **Behaviour:** Primarily terrestrial, uses fallen timber as pathways. Solitary, but may feed in groups. Crepuscular. **Diet:** Fruit, insects, seeds, fungi.

Breeding: October to April, 1–3 young. Mature at just over 2 years. **Features:** Soft, dense fur is rich brown flecked with darker hairs, slightly paler below; sometimes has white patches on chest and throat. Thin tail is dark brown and scaly. Hind foot has opposable first toe. Female has 4 teats.

Length: ♂ HB 153–273 mm, T 132–159 mm; ♀ HB 212–252 mm, T 123–153 mm.
Weight: ♂ 360–680 g; ♀ 453–635 g.
Status: Secure in limited habitat.

Stan Breeden

Rufous Hare-wallaby
Lagorchestes hirsutus

✘ The Banded Hare-wallaby belongs to the subfamily Sthenurinae; the other species to the Macropodinae.

✘ The Central and Eastern Hare-wallabies are presumed extinct.

✘ By 1991 the last of the Rufous Hare-wallabies in the Tanami Desert had been wiped out by foxes, drought and bushfire.

✘ The temperature inside a hare-wallaby's spinifex hummock tunnel seldom rises above 30°C.

Location Tips

→ Mt Isa, Qld
→ Borroloola,Tanami Desert, NT

Hare-wallabies

The hare-wallaby is an outback version of the compact macropod. It is a water-efficient model with a temperature-control system designed for harsh conditions.

Hare-wallabies are found in arid and semi-arid habitats where grass and low shrubs offer protective cover. Their daytime refuges include scraped-out hollows under bushes and tunnels made in or underneath tussock or hummock grass. To escape the summer heat, they sometimes dig short burrows that can be up to 700 millimetres deep. They leave their cool retreats at night to browse on leaves, grass tips and fleshy succulents. Their food supplies all the water they need as they produce little urine and do not turn on the body's evaporative cooling system until the air temperature exceeds 30°C.

Breeding occurs throughout the year, but there are usually two peak periods that coincide with seasonal rain. After a one-month gestation period, the female gives birth and mates again. Development of the resultant embryo is delayed until the current joey vacates the pouch at four to five months of age, or, if food is scarce, for the duration of drought conditions.

The Banded Hare-wallaby is the only member of its subfamily, Sthenurinae, and is but distantly related to the "true" hare-wallabies, subfamily Macropodinae.

Camouflage colours help protect the Rufous Hare-wallaby from birds of prey.

Spectacled Hare-wallaby
Lagorchestes conspicillatus
(spectacled dancing-hare)

Named for the reddish rings around its eyes, it is found in mainland tropical grassland and on Barrow Island, Western Australia. Its populations have declined, though not as drastically as other hare-wallabies, because of habitat change and depredation by Feral Cats.

Habitat: Open forest and woodland shrubs, tussock and hummock grasses.
Behaviour: Terrestrial, solitary, nocturnal. **Diet:** Shrubs, grass. **Breeding:** All year, 1 young. Mature by 1 year.
Features: Grey-brown flecked with white above, white below, pale stripe on hip. Black nose. Orange eye rings. Feet are grey-brown. Sparsely furred tail has dark tip. Female has 4 teats.
Length: HB 400–470 mm, T 370–490 mm.
Weight: 1.6–4.5 kg. **Status:** Secure.

Ian Morris

Rufous Hare-wallaby *Lagorchestes hirsutus* (hairy dancing-hare)

The Rufous Hare-wallaby, also known as the Mala, was common in the western deserts until the 1930s. It is now restricted to Bernier and Dorre Islands off Shark Bay, Western Australia. Attempts are underway to re-establish a population in the Tanami Desert.

Habitat: Spinifex grassland and coastal shrubland. **Behaviour:** Terrestrial, solitary, nocturnal. **Diet:** Shrubs, herbs, grass, seeds, insects. **Breeding:** All year, 1 young. Females mature at 5 months, males by 14 months. **Features:** Reddish fur with grey-brown tinge on back, darker on head. White moustache below black nose. Sparsely furred tail darkens towards tip. Female has 4 teats.
Length: ♂ HB 310–360 mm, T 260–280 mm; ♀ HB 360–390 mm, T 245–305 mm.
Weight: ♂ 1250–1800 g; ♀ 780–1960 g.
Status: Endangered.

Red-necked Pademelon
Thylogale thetis

Location Tips

→ Maiala NP, Qld
→ Mt Field NP, Tas
→ Washpool NP, NSW
→ Wilsons Promontory
NP, Vic

Pademelons

Pademelons are the resident macropods of Australia's eastern forests. Their low-slung, compact bodies are ideal for travelling through thick undergrowth. They move quickly with short, bouncy hops while holding in the arms and extending the tail straight behind the body. When resting, a pademelon swings its short, thick tail between its legs, sits on the base of the tail and leans back against a tree or rock.

Pademelons shelter and forage in the forest, and do most of their eating from late afternoon to early morning. They use a network of runways when moving to and from their feeding grounds, and may travel several kilometres in a night.

They are timid creatures that rarely stray far from the edges of the forest. When frightened, a pademelon will thump its hind feet to warn its feeding companions, then bolt for safety.

These knee-high macropods will accept human company when fed regularly and may approach visitors at picnic and camping grounds.

Tasmanian Pademelon *Thylogale billardierii* (Billardière's pouched-weasel)

Tasmanian Pademelons, now confined to Tasmania and the larger islands of Bass Strait, used to exist on the mainland but fell victim to the fur and leather trade. They were also a food item favoured by Aborigines and Europeans.

Habitat: Rainforest, wet eucalypt forest, tea-tree scrub, damp or well-vegetated areas of open woodland. **Behaviour:** Terrestrial, mainly solitary, nocturnal. **Diet:** Grass, herbs, leaves. **Breeding:** All year with a peak in autumn, 1 young. Mature by 14 months. **Features:** Thick fur is dark brown to grey-brown above, reddish-tinged buff underneath and inside ears. Short face. Short, thick tail is about ⅔ head and body length. Female has 4 teats.

Length: ♂ HB up to 630 mm, T 345–483 mm; ♀ HB up to 560 mm, T 320 mm. **Weight:** ♂ 3.8–12 kg; ♀ 2.4–10 kg. **Status:** Secure.

Red-legged Pademelon *Thylogale stigmatica* (pricked [pattern] pouched-weasel)

This pademelon's distribution extends farther north than does that of the Red-necked Pademelon. The female calls her wayward young with a soft "tsk" sound; when rejecting a suitor, she issues a harsh rasp. Adults thump the ground with the hind feet to signal an alarm.

Habitat: Rainforest, wet eucalypt forest, monsoon vine forest.
Behaviour: Terrestrial, mainly solitary, rests early afternoon and around midnight.
Diet: Leaves, fruit. **Breeding:** All year, 1 young. Females mature at 7 months; males at 10 months. **Features:** Soft, thick fur is grey-brown above, cream to pale grey below. Cheeks, arms and legs are red-tinged. Rainforest dwellers have darker fur. Female has 4 teats.
Length: ♂ HB 470–536 mm,
 T 372–473 mm;
 ♀ HB 386–520 mm,
 T 301–445 mm.
Weight: ♂ 3.7–6.8 kg;
 ♀ 2.5–4.1 kg.
Status: Secure.

Red-necked Pademelon
Thylogale thetis (Thétis [Bougainville's ship] pouched-weasel)

This small macropod inhabits forest edges and is sometimes considered a pest when agricultural land abuts the forest.

Habitat: Rainforest, wet eucalypt forest.
Behaviour: Terrestrial, mainly solitary, most active late afternoon to early morning.
Diet: Grass, shrubs. **Breeding:** All year, 1 young. Females mature by 17 months.
Features: Thick soft fur is brownish grey above with red tinge on neck and shoulders. Belly, chest and chin are pale. Female has 4 teats.
Length: ♂ HB 300–620 mm, T 270–510 mm; ♀ HB 290–500 mm; T 270–370 mm.
Weight: ♂ 2.5–9.1 kg;
 ♀ 1.8–4.3 kg.
Status: Secure.

Quokka

The Quokka is the only species in its genus and is regarded rather as a durable but superseded model in the evolution of typical macropods. In 1696, Dutch navigator Willem de Vlamingh mistakenly identified the Quokka as a large rat and named its island home Rottnest (rat nest). Until the 1960s it was also common in the wetter parts of south-west Western Australia. It is now found in isolated populations south of Perth.

Quokkas live in groups dominated by the oldest males which aggressively defend their resting places but are quite content to eat and drink with the rankless females and juveniles. Quokkas browse on leaves and will climb low bushes to reach food. Their survival also depends on fresh drinking water, and group territories centre around available sources.

Quokkas will delay breeding if conditions are too hot and dry. After a joey vacates the pouch at about 26 weeks of age, it continues to suckle while learning to forage with its mother.

The Quokka looks very much like other small wallabies except for having a comparatively short, thick tail.

Location Tips

→ Rottnest Island, WA
→ Stirling Range NP, WA
→ Wellington Dam near Collie, WA

Quokka *Setonix brachyurus* (bristle-footed short-tail)

On Rottnest Island, groups of up to 150 congregate around freshwater soaks during dry summers. Isolated mainland populations are making a comeback in swampy areas where introduced predators are controlled.

Habitat: Coastal shrubland, heath, eucalypt forest and woodland with shrubby understorey.
Behaviour: Terrestrial, gregarious, active day and night; has well-developed social structure.
Diet: Grass, leaves and succulent plants; often malnourished by summer's end on Rottnest.

Breeding: January or March on Rottnest Island, all year on mainland; 1 young. Mature by 2 years. **Lifespan:** Up to 10 years. **Features:** Robust, compact body. Coarse, thick fur is grey-brown tinged with red, but has no definite body markings. Ears are small and round. Forehead may have a dark stripe. Short, thick tail is sparsely furred and has visible scales. Bristly hairs on toes. Female has 4 teats.
Length: ♂ HB 435–540 mm, T 260–310 mm; ♀ HB 400–500 mm, T 245–285 mm.
Weight: ♂ 2.7–4.2 kg; ♀ 2.7–3.5 kg.
Status: Secure.

Swamp Wallaby

Zoologists classify the Swamp Wallaby as the only member of the genus *Wallabia*. Being more of a browser than a grazer, it prefers habitats with a dense understorey. It is more diurnal than most macropods, resting and foraging amongst the undergrowth during the day, and moving out to more open feeding grounds at night. Unlike other wallabies, it has extra large premolars with sharp cutting edges.

Its hopping gait is different, too, with the head held lower and the tail extending straight behind the body.

Breeding is much the same as for other macropods, except that the female mates a second time before giving birth so that pregnancies overlap. A joey vacates its mother's pouch by nine months of age to make way for the embryo-in-waiting, but continues to suckle for another six months.

While typical wallabies have 16 chromosomes, the male Swamp Wallaby has only 11 and the female 10.

Like other wallabies and kangaroos, the first toe on the hind foot is missing and only the fourth and fifth toes touch the ground when the animal moves.

Location Tips

→ Great Sandy NP, Qld
→ Royal NP, NSW
→ Grampians NP, Vic

Swamp Wallaby
Wallabia bicolor (two-coloured wallaby)

The Swamp Wallaby exploits a variety of habitats, but is the largest macropod found in dense coastal heath. It can be distinguished from other wallabies by its dark colour.

Habitat: Forest, woodland, brigalow scrub, coastal heath. **Behaviour:** Terrestrial, solitary, mostly nocturnal. **Diet:** Grass, ferns, shrubs. **Breeding:** All year, 1 young. Mature at 15–18 months. **Lifespan:** Up to 15 years. **Features:** Coarse fur is dark brown to charcoal above, tinged yellow to red-orange below. Dark face with pale yellow or light brown cheek stripe. Dark paws. Dark tail sometimes has white tip.
Length: ♂ HB 723–847 mm,
T 690–862 mm;
♀ 665–750 mm, T 640–728 mm.
Weight: ♂ 12.3–20.5 kg; ♀ 10.3–15.4 kg.
Status: Secure.

Lumholtz's Tree-kangaroo
Dendrolagus lumholtzi

✘ Australia's two species of tree-kangaroo live in wet tropical rainforests in northern Queensland.

✘ A frightened tree-kangaroo can leap to the ground from as high as 15 metres.

✘ Fifty-thousand-year-old fossils of a tree-kangaroo as large as a Red Kangaroo have been found in NSW.

✘ The Bennett's Tree-kangaroo makes a loud, rasping sound when alarmed.

✘ Male tree-kangaroos aggressively defend their territories from each other.

Tree-kangaroos

Tree-kangaroos are an unusual group of macropods that have returned to their ancestral home in the forest canopy. Their success as tree-dwellers probably has more to do with the absence of similar-sized predators and competitors than with their climbing ability.

These medium-sized macropods have longer arms and shorter hind feet than a typical kangaroo. Opposable thumbs and recurved claws on the front paws provide grip, while textured soles on the rectangular hind feet give non-slip traction. A tree-kangaroo's hind legs can move independently of one another, so it can walk on all fours backwards and forwards. When hopping along a branch or on the ground, the long, non-prehensile tail is held behind the body as a counterbalance. A tree-kangaroo descends from a tree tail-first. The front paws move alternately while the hind feet slide against the trunk. About two metres from the ground it pushes off, executes a mid-air twist and finishes with an upright landing.

Tree-kangaroos move through the canopy at night in search of leaves and fruit. The day is spent resting on a sturdy branch. They usually live alone, but are sometimes seen feeding in small groups.

It is thought that tree-kangaroos took to the trees in search of food and in the absence of predators or competitors.

Bennett's Tree-kangaroo *Dendrolagus bennettianus* (Bennett's tree-hare)

Bennett's Tree-kangaroo is the largest tree-dwelling mammal in Australia. The young are independent at nine months, but stay with their mothers for up to two years. The male occupies a territory of about 25 hectares, which takes in the smaller territories of several females. Males fight savagely to defend their territories.

Habitat: Highland and lowland tropical rainforest, vine forest. **Behaviour:** Mostly arboreal, solitary, nocturnal. **Diet:** Leaves, fruit. **Breeding:** All year, 1 young. **Features:** Dark brown above, fawn below. Face is grey. Shoulders, and back of head and neck, are rusty brown. Feet are black. Female has 4 teats.
Length: ♂ HB 720–750 mm, T 820–840 mm; ♀ HB 690–705 mm; T 730–800 mm.
Weight: ♂ 11.5–13.7 kg; ♀ 8–10.6 kg.
Status: Secure.

Lumholtz's Tree-kangaroo
Dendrolagus lumholtzi (Lumholtz's tree-hare)

This tree-kangaroo is found in highland rainforest between Mt Spurgeon and the Cardwell Range in Queensland. Rainforest trees are its main source of food, although it sometimes browses on crops near the forest edges.

Habitat: Highland tropical rainforest.
Behaviour: Mostly arboreal, solitary, nocturnal.
Diet: Leaves, fruit. **Breeding:** All year, 1 young.
Features: Blackish brown above with paler rump. Face, feet and last half of tail are dark. Light stripe across forehead and on cheeks. Female has 4 teats.
Length: ♂ HB 520–650 mm, T 655–736 mm;
♀ HB 533–603 mm, T 670–732 mm.
Weight: ♂ 5.4–8.6 kg; ♀ 5.1–7.0 kg.
Status: Secure.

Brush-tailed Rock-wallaby
Petrogale penicillata

✘ Female rock-wallabies tend to be a third smaller than males.

✘ Aborigines used pit traps to catch rock-wallabies and the elders controlled distribution of the meat.

✘ Rock-wallabies live for up to 8 years in the wild.

✘ The Purple-necked Rock-wallaby secretes a water-soluble pigment that stains the fur on its face and neck.

✘ Feral goats compete with rock-wallabies for food and shelter.

Rock-wallabies

Rock-wallabies may not be able to leap tall buildings in a single bound, but they make scaling a cliff-face seem effortless. While most of these macropods are no more than half a metre tall, their speed and grace is awe-inspiring.

These accomplished rock-hoppers are equipped with powerful spring-loaded hind legs and thick, textured soles for maximum traction, as well as flexible, muscular tails for stability and steering control.

The rocky outcrops, gorges and escarpments of Australia's ancient mountains and eroded plateaus are the favoured haunts of rock-wallabies. They shelter in crevices and caves, and browse among the rocks or descend to graze on the edges of open grassy areas. Grass makes up most of their diet, but they also feed on leaves and fruit. A specialised stomach helps them digest this fibrous plant food.

Grooming and sunbathing are regular daytime activities for Black-footed Rock-wallabies.

Life in the Colonies

Rock-wallabies live in colonies and the number of individuals in each colony depends on the availability of food and shelter. In some species, social interactions are limited to mating encounters and shared feeding areas.

Colonial life for a Yellow-footed Rock-wallaby is a more rigid affair. Each group within a large Yellow-foot colony consists of a dominant male, several females and juveniles, and a few subservient males. The leader has exclusive breeding rights and maintains his dominance by hissing, stamping, chasing and occasional physical violence.

Female rock-wallabies can breed throughout the year, but most young are produced when conditions are favourable. As with other macropods, the female carries an embryo-in-waiting, which is born a few weeks before the incumbent joey permanently vacates her pouch. The newly weaned juvenile learns the finer points of rock-hopping at its mother's heels, but is left in a cave or crevice while she looks for food.

When feeding and basking, rock-wallabies will stand up to investigate noises, ready to make a bounding retreat if alarmed. Their size, agility and camouflage colours offer some protection from predators that invade their rocky domains. However, they are defenceless on open ground.

Mareeba Rock-wallabies are social animals that share their feeding sites.

Finding Rock-wallabies

Look for movement on rock faces and listen for the distinctive slap of their feet on rocks.

Look for smoothly polished rocks that indicate a regular runway.

Droppings are oval or cylindrical pellets usually in groups of 4 to 8.

Scan rock faces carefully as rock-wallabies are well camouflaged and reluctant to move when basking on cool winter mornings.

Look in grassy areas at the base of rocky outcrops during late afternoon.

Location Tips

→ Gammon Ranges, SA
→ Idalia NP, Qld
→ Mutawintji NP, NSW
→ Macdonnell Ranges, NT
→ Grampians NP, Vic
→ Kalbarri NP, WA

✘ The Nabarlek is the only macropod to have replaceable molar teeth.

✘ In 1908, a Sydney fur trader sold 92,500 Brush-tailed Rock-wallaby skins.

✘ The Yellow-foots were hunted for sport in the Flinders Ranges, South Australia, until 1912.

Time and Change

Fossils reveal rock-wallabies once migrated long distances between suitable habitats. Now that much of the land between rocky outcrops is cleared and fenced for agriculture and grazing, their wandering days are over.

When separate colonies of the same species of rock-wallaby cannot cross open spaces safely, there is little opportunity to interbreed. So nature works with the genetic material that is available, and the members of each colony develop features to suit conditions in their particular habitat. Eventually the wallabies of separate groups become distinct species – there are so many physical differences that breeding across groups will not produce viable offspring, even when given the chance.

Ian Morris

Black-footed Rock-wallabies blend in well with their semi-arid, rocky habitat.

Power-boosted hind legs propel a Mareeba Rock-wallaby's extraordinary leap across a granite crevice.

Allied Rock-wallaby *Petrogale assimilis* (similar rock-weasel)

This Queensland rock-wallaby's distribution spreads west from Home Hill to Croydon and Hughenden near the southern boundary of the wet tropics. The species is also found on Palm and Magnetic Islands. Pair bonding between the sexes is maintained by grooming and sharing of feeding and daytime resting sites.

Habitat: Open eucalypt forest and woodland.
Behaviour: Terrestrial, gregarious, mostly nocturnal. **Diet:** Grass, leaves, fruit.
Breeding: All year, 1 young. Mature at 18 months. **Lifespan:** Up to 13 years.
Features: Dark brown to grey-brown, buff coloured belly, forearms, hind legs and tail base. Pale cheek stripe and sometimes dark stripe on forehead. Dark feet, brushy tail-tip.
Length: ♂ HB 470–590 mm, T 409–545 mm; ♀ HB 445–550 mm, T 445–550 mm.
Weight: ♂ 4.7 kg; ♀ 4.3 kg.
Status: Secure.

Short-eared Rock-wallaby *Petrogale brachyotis* (short-eared rock-weasel)

The Short-eared Rock-wallaby usually lives near permanent water and relies on monsoon rains to renew its food supplies. It is found from the Kimberley around to the Gulf of Carpentaria in areas where rainfall exceeds 700 millimetres per year. Often the only signs of its presence are lots of small droppings on the rocks.

Habitat: Tropical woodland and grassland.
Behaviour: Terrestrial, gregarious, nocturnal.
Diet: Grass, leaves, fruit and seeds.
Breeding: Possibly all year, 1 young.
Features: Short, fine fur varies from uniform light grey to dark grey or brown above. Dark stripe from forehead to between shoulders. May have white or dark neck stripe, or pale side and hip stripes. Short ears are uniform colour with white margins.
Length: ♂ HB 435–550 mm, T 387–550 mm;
♀ HB 405–485 mm, T 320–520 mm.
Weight: ♂ 3.2–5.6 kg; ♀ 2.2–4.7 kg.
Status: Secure.

Ian Morris

Monjon *Petrogale burbidgei* (Burbidge's rock-weasel)

The Monjon, also known as the Warabi, is the smallest of the rock-wallabies. It is found in rugged sandstone country along parts of the Kimberley coastline in Western Australia, and on the nearby islands of the Bonaparte Archipelago.

Habitat: Open woodland with eucalypts and acacias. **Behaviour:** Terrestrial, gregarious, mostly nocturnal. **Diet:** Grass, leaves, fruit. **Breeding:** Possibly all year, 1 young. **Features:** Olive marbled with fawn and black, fawn underneath with yellow-tinged flanks. Indistinct pale stripe from snout to base of ear. Pale midline stripe on head and neck. Olive-grey tail with bushy tip. Short ears. Black foot pads. **Length:** HB 306–353 mm, T 264–290 mm. **Weight:** 960–1430 g. **Status:** Secure.

Jiri Lochman, Lochman Transparencies

Nabarlek *Petrogale concinna* (elegant rock-weasel)

This small rock-wallaby inhabits sandstone outcrops on the coastal plains of northern Australia. It is the only macropod to have an unlimited number of molar teeth: these erupt and move forward in the jaw as worn-down teeth are lost. The plants eaten are rich in silica and so are very abrasive on teeth.

Habitat: Woodland. **Behaviour:** Terrestrial, gregarious, mostly nocturnal. **Diet:** Grass, ferns. **Breeding:** All year with a peak in the wet season, 1 young. Mature by 2 years. **Features:** Fur is dull red, marbled with grey, black above, sometimes with a darker shoulder stripe, and greyish white below. Tail has dark and brushy tip. **Length:** HB 290–350 mm, T 220–310 mm. **Weight:** 1.0–1.7 kg. **Status:** Vulnerable.

Ian Morris

Black-footed Rock-wallaby
Petrogale lateralis (notable-sided rock-weasel)

This wallaby's common name is a little confusing for wildlife watchers because it is the bottom of its feet, not the top, that is black. Males and females in a colony have separate pecking orders. This is a genetically diverse species which currently includes four different races. The Macdonnell Ranges race is described below.

Habitat: Rocky outcrops with deep fissures and caves.
Behaviour: Terrestrial, gregarious, mostly nocturnal.
Diet: Grasses and some leaves and fruits.
Features: Dark grey-brown above, light-coloured cheek stripe, dark stripe from between ears to beyond shoulders, white side stripe, dark grey to brown tail.
Length: HB 450–521 mm,
T 507–597 mm. **Weight:** 2.8–4.5 kg.
Status: Common in parts of range.

Mareeba Rock-wallaby *Petrogale mareeba* (Mareeba rock-weasel)

This cryptic rock-wallaby obtained its status as a species in 1992. It is found among granite and basalt outcrops on the Atherton Tableland and is commonly seen at Granite Gorge.

Habitat: Open forest. **Behaviour:** Terrestrial, gregarious, mostly nocturnal.
Diet: Grass and leaves.
Breeding: Possibly all year, 1 young.
Features: Usually grey-brown above, but may be dark brown to almost black, depending on habitat. Paler underside, forearms, hind legs and tail base. May have pale cheek and forehead stripes. Tail darkens towards the bushy end, which may have a grey-white tip.
Length: ♂ HB 425–548 mm,
T 420–530 mm;
♀ 425–500 mm,
T 415–467 mm.
Weight: ♂ 4.5 kg; ♀ 3.8 kg.
Status: Secure.

Brush-tailed Rock-wallaby
Petrogale penicillata (brush[-tailed] rock-weasel)

Populations of Brush-tailed Rock-wallabies are scattered along the Great Dividing Range from southern Queensland to The Grampians in Victoria. It prefers the north face of rocky outcrops where it can bask.

Habitat: Eucalypt forest with grass understorey.
Behaviour: Terrestrial, gregarious, mostly nocturnal.
Diet: Grass, soft leaves, fruit, seeds, flowers.
Features: Coarse, shaggy fur is brown above with reddish neck, shoulders and rump. Underside is paler, sometimes with white chest blaze. May have pale grey side stripe with darker stripe below. White cheek stripe and black stripe from forehead to back of head. Feet and last part of bushy tail are

dark brown to black. Ears slightly yellow inside, black outside. **Length:** ♂ 529–586 mm, T 510–700 mm; ♀ HB 510–570 mm, T 500–630 mm. **Weight:** ♂ 5.5–10.9 kg; ♀ 4.9–8.2 kg. **Status:** Vulnerable.

Proserpine Rock-wallaby
Petrogale persephone (Proserpine rock-weasel)

This species is found in Queensland around Proserpine,
Airlie Beach and on some islands of the Whitsundays.
Males can weigh 60% more than females.

Habitat: Coastal forest with nearby open grassy
woodland. **Behaviour:** Terrestrial, gregarious, mostly
nocturnal. **Diet:** Grass, leaves. **Breeding:** Possibly all
year, 1 young. **Features:** Dark greyish brown flecked
with white, rufous shoulders and tail base, pale cheek
stripe with slightly darker stripe below. Ears black inside,
brownish orange outside. White chin and throat, pale
yellow belly, dark paws. Dark tail may have yellowish
white tip. Predominantly grey during autumn moult.
Length: ♂ HB 501–640 mm,
T 580–676 mm;
♀ HB 526–630 mm, T 515–624 mm.
Weight: ♂ 5.6–6.8 kg; ♀ 4.1–6.4 kg.
Status: Endangered.

Ian Morris

Yellow-footed Rock-wallaby
Petrogale xanthopus (yellow-footed rock-weasel)

This is the largest of the rock-wallabies and is found in
semi-arid habitats. It is best known from the Flinders
Ranges, South Australia, but a substantial population
lives in the ranges south-west of Blackall, Queensland.

Habitat: Open woodland.
Behaviour: Terrestrial, gregarious, mostly nocturnal.
Diet: Grass, leaves.
Breeding: All year, 1 young. Females mature at
1–2 years; males at 2.5 years.
Features: Fawn-grey above, white below. Rich brown
stripe from crown to mid back. White stripe on cheek,
side and thigh. Brown stripe on shoulder and upper
thigh. Ears, arms, legs and tail are orange-
yellow. Tail has dark bands.
Length: HB 480–650 mm, T 565–700 mm.
Weight: 6–12 kg.
Status: Vulnerable in SA and NSW.

Bridled Nailtail
Wallaby
Onychogalea fraenata

✘ Nailtail wallabies
have three pairs
of slender upper
incisors.

✘ Nailtail wallabies
were called "organ-
grinders" because
their forearms make
circular motions
when they hop.

✘ When hopping
quickly, a nailtail
wallaby's tail curves
upward.

✘ Nailtail wallabies
will scrape aside
leaf litter to expose
tender plant shoots.

Location Tips

→ Idalia NP, Qld
→ Barkly Tableland,
NT
→ East Kimberley, WA

Nailtail Wallabies

These shy, attractive wallabies with their slender faces and
distinctive markings were named after the small, horny spur on
the ends of their tails. The spur appears to have no function.

Of the three species that once thrived in Australia's semi-arid
shrubland and grassy woodland, only the Northern Nailtail
Wallaby remains common. The Crescent Nailtail is presumed
extinct and the Bridled Nailtail has retreated to a small area
near Dingo in Queensland. Being selective browsers and
grazers, nailtail wallabies have not been able to compete with
the indiscriminate appetites of stock, Feral Goats and Rabbits.

Nailtail wallabies rest alone during the day in a scraped-out
depression at the base of a dense shrub or a clump of grass.
They emerge just before dusk to feed in small groups in more
open areas. When disturbed, a nailtail wallaby will drop flat on
the ground or crawl quietly back into the scrub.

This Bridled Nailtail rests, camouflaged, in a clump of grass.

Bridled Nailtail Wallaby
Onychogalea fraenata (bridled nailed-weasel)

The population of Bridled Nailtail Wallabies at Taunton Scientific Reserve in Queensland has increased almost tenfold since cattle were excluded from their habitat.

Habitat: Open eucalypt forest, grassy woodland, shrubland. **Behaviour:** Terrestrial, mostly solitary but 4 or 5 may graze together, mostly nocturnal.
Diet: Grass, soft ground plants, shrubs. **Breeding:** All year with a spring–summer peak, 1 young. **Features:** Grey-brown flecked with white to brownish fawn. Paler flanks and underside. Rufous-tinged shoulders. White "bridle" stripe from back of neck to underarm. Dark stripe from nose to eye, a pale cheek stripe to below eye. Dark stripe from forehead to mid back. Long, slender ears. **Length:** ♂ HB 510–700 mm, T 380–540 mm; ♀ HB 430–540 mm, T 360–440 mm.
Weight: ♂ 5–8 kg; ♀ 4–5 kg.
Status: Endangered.

Northern Nailtail Wallaby
Onychogalea unguifera (nail-bearing nailed-weasel)

This nailtail wallaby's range extends from inland grass plains to coastal floodplains. They may travel several kilometres when feeding at night, but remain close to cover.

Habitat: Open woodland, shrubland, tussock grassland. **Behaviour:** Terrestrial, mostly solitary, mostly nocturnal. **Diet:** Small ground plants, succulents, fruit, grass shoots.
Breeding: Possibly all year, 1 young.
Features: Sandy fur with dark stripe from mid back to tail. May have pale cheek and hip stripes. Tail may have dark bands and dark tufted tip. Long slender ears.
Length: ♂ HB 540–690 mm; T 600–730 mm; ♀ HB 490–600 mm, T 600–650 mm.
Weight: ♂ 6–9 kg, ♀ 4.5–7 kg.
Status: Secure.

Ian Morris

Eastern Grey Kangaroos *Macropus giganteus*

✗ There are 13 living species of macropods in the genus *Macropus*.

✗ The Toolache Wallaby is presumed extinct.

✗ Adult male kangaroos are larger and have longer, more muscular arms than females.

✗ Eastern and Western Grey Kangaroos sometimes live in the same mob.

✗ Kangaroos, wallaroos and wallabies are protected by legislation, but may be culled under permit if they are considered a pest to crops and pastures.

Kangaroos, Wallaroos and Typical Wallabies

Kangaroos, wallaroos and wallabies belonging to the genus *Macropus* are Australia's most common and easily recognised macropods. These adaptable, energy efficient herbivores are also the most diverse, abundant and widespread group of marsupials. Several of the open range species have increased in number and distribution in the past 200 years with the grazing industry providing additional sources of food and water.

Living with the Mob

Many of these macropods live in extended family groups within large mobs. A group usually consists of a dominant male, several females and their young. Young males of breeding age tend to form separate groups, while battle-worn old males often choose to live alone. Adult males challenge one another to establish their rank in the mob hierarchy. The higher a male's status, the more females will mate with him. Sparring involves holding on, raking an opponent's head and chest with sharp claws and kicking with the hind legs.

Even the most solitary species sometimes feed in pairs and family threesomes, or, in the case of Red-necked Wallabies, more than 30 individuals may gather at a prime feeding site.

Eastern Grey Kangaroos form large mobs when food is plentiful.

Red Kangaroo

What's the Difference?

Kangaroo is a general term for large grazing macropods. It also is used as a name for the Red, Eastern Grey and Western Grey Kangaroos.

Wallaroos are basically kangaroos that live in hilly or rocky country. They have large, bare, black noses. Wallaroos have a distinctive upright stance with shoulders thrown back, elbows tucked into the sides and wrists raised.

Wallaby is a common word used to distinguish medium-sized macropods from larger kangaroos. Wallabies weigh less than 25 kilograms and, being smaller, most rely on the protective shelter of habitats with dense undergrowth.

Red-necked Wallaby

Juvenile Common Wallaroo

Agile Wallaby *Macropus agilis* (agile long-foot)

This social wallaby, the most common in tropical coastal Australia and south-eastern lowland Papua New Guinea, lives in groups of up to 10 and several groups will form a mob when feeding. It is known to dig up grass roots from 30 centimetres below the surface.

Habitat: Open forest, woodland, grassland. **Behaviour:** Terrestrial, gregarious, active late

afternoon to early morning. **Diet:** Grass, sedges, leaves, fruit. **Breeding:** All year, 30 days gestation, pouch life of 7–8 months. Weaned at 10–12 months. Females mature at 12 months, males at 14 months. **Features:** Sandy brown above, whitish below. Dark stripe on forehead. Light stripe on cheeks and thighs. Black ear edges and tail tip. **Length:** ♂ HB 715–850 mm, T 692–840 mm; ♀ HB 593–722 mm, T 587–700 mm. **Weight:** ♂ 16–27 kg; ♀ 9–15 kg. **Status:** Secure.

Black-striped Wallaby *Macropus dorsalis* (notably-backed long-foot)

Groups of 20 or more Black-striped Wallabies rest in permanent camps during the day. They file out at dusk to feed along the forest edges and on open ground. Even when alarmed the group does not split up.

Habitat: Forest and woodland with shrub undergrowth. **Behaviour:** Terrestrial, gregarious, nocturnal. **Diet:** Grass, leaves.

Breeding: Gestation 33–35 days, pouch life of 7 months. Females mature at 14 months, males at 20 months. **Lifespan:** Up to 15 years. **Features:** Brown above with reddish tinge to upper back and arms, greyish white below. Black stripe from forehead to rump. White stripe on cheeks and thighs. Scaly, sparsely furred tail. **Length:** ♂ HB 680–820 mm, T 740–830 mm; ♀ HB 530–615 mm, T 540–615 mm. **Weight:** ♂ Up to 20 kg; ♀ 6–8 kg. **Status:** Secure.

Tammar Wallaby
Macropus eugenii (Eugene Island long-foot)

Most Tammars are found on islands; however, there are a few mainland populations. Those in semi-arid habitats have been observed drinking seawater.

Habitat: Dry eucalypt forest, woodland, shrubland, heath. **Behaviour:** Terrestrial, solitary, but may feed in groups, nocturnal. **Diet:** Grass, leaves. **Breeding:** December to March, pouch life of 8–9 months. Females mature at 9 months, males at 2 years. **Lifespan:** Up to 14 years. **Features:** Dark grey-brown with white flecks. Red-tinged flanks and limbs. Pale grey to buff below. **Length*:** ♂ HB 590–680 mm, T 380–450 mm; ♀ HB 520–630 mm, T 330–440 mm. **Weight*:** ♂ 6–10 kg; ♀ 4–6 kg. **Status:** Secure.

*Kangaroo Island population.

Western Brush Wallaby
Macropus irma (Irma's long-foot)

The Western Brush Wallaby moves through open woodland with speed and agility, keeping its body low to the ground and its tail extended.

Habitat: Open forest and woodland with low understorey of grass and shrubs, sometimes in heathland. **Behaviour:** Terrestrial, solitary, active in late afternoon and early morning. **Diet:** Grass. **Breeding:** Possibly March to May, pouch life of 6–7 months. **Features:** Pale grey, sometimes with brown tinge. White stripe from nose to base of ear, black-rimmed ears. Paws and last half of crested tail are black. Some have bands on back and tail. **Length:** HB 1200 mm, T 540–970 mm. **Weight:** 7–9 kg. **Status:** Secure.

Jiri Lochman, Lochman Transparencies

Parma Wallaby *Macropus parma* ([indigenous name] long-foot)

The Parma Wallaby was thought to be extinct by the 1960s and some were repatriated from New Zealand for captive breeding programs. The species occurs naturally in New South Wales from the Watagan Mountains to Gibraltar Range.

Habitat: Eucalypt forest, sometimes rainforest. **Behaviour:** Terrestrial, solitary but may feed in pairs, nocturnal. **Diet:** Grass, herbs. **Breeding:** January to June, gestation about 35 days,

pouch life of 30 weeks, weaned 10–14 weeks later. Females mature at 1 year; males at 2 years. **Features:** Pale grey-brown. White chest and throat. White cheek stripe to below eye. Dark stripe from forehead to mid back. May have white-tipped tail. **Length:** ♂ HB 482–528 mm, T 489–544 mm; ♀ HB 447–527 mm, T 405–507 mm. **Weight:** ♂ 4.1–5.9 kg; ♀ 3.2–4.8 kg. **Status:** Vulnerable.

Allan Fox

Whiptail Wallaby *Macropus parryi* (Parry's long-foot)

This beautiful macropod is found in hilly country in Queensland and northern New South Wales. It lives in mobs of up to 50 where dominant males maintain control by ritualised aggression that includes pulling up clumps of grass. Foot thumping is used to warn others of danger.

Habitat: Open eucalypt forest with grass understorey. **Behaviour:** Terrestrial, gregarious, least active in the middle of the day. **Diet:** Grass, herbs, ferns. **Breeding:** Gestation 34–38 days, pouch life of 37 weeks, weaned at 15 months. Females mature by 2 years, males at 2–3 years. **Features:** Light grey to brownish grey above, white below. Face and base of ears are dark brown. White cheek stripe. Light brown stripe from neck to shoulder. Long, slender tail has dark tip.
Length: ♂ HB up to 924 mm, T 861–1045 mm; ♀ HB up to 755 mm, T 728–858 mm **Weight:** ♂ 14–26 kg; ♀ 7–15 kg. **Status:** Secure.

Red-necked Wallaby
Macropus rufogriseus (red-grey long-foot)

The mainland subspecies of this wallaby, *Macropus rufogriseus banksianus,* shelters amid dense shrubs and emerges late afternoon to feed in open grassy areas along the forest edges.

Habitat: Eucalypt forest, coastal heath.
Behaviour: Terrestrial, solitary but feeds in groups, active from late afternoon but earlier on dull or cool days. **Diet:** Grass, herbs, shrubbery.
Breeding: All year with a slight peak in summer. Gestation about 30 days, pouch life of 280 days, weaned at 12–17 months. Females mature earlier than males. **Features:** Grizzled grey-brown to reddish brown above with red tinge to neck, pale grey to white below. Snout and paws are black. Pale stripe on upper lip.
Length: ♂ HB 770–888 mm, T 703–876 mm; ♀ 708–837 mm, T 664–790 mm.
Weight: ♂ 15–23.7 kg; ♀ 12–15.5 kg.
Status: Secure.

The Bass Strait islands and Tasmanian subspecies, *Macropus rufogriseus rufogriseus,* is commonly known as Bennett's Wallaby.

Habitat: Forest, woodland, shrubland.
Behaviour: Terrestrial, mostly solitary but feeds in groups, active from late afternoon but earlier on overcast or cool days. **Diet:** Grass, herbs, shrubbery.
Breeding: One season, births occur from late January to July. Gestation about 30 days, pouch life of 280 days, weaned at 12–17 months. Females mature earlier than males. **Features:** Similar to mainland Red-necked Wallaby, but has longer, darker fur and browner neck.
Length: ♂ HB 712–923 mm, T 691–862 mm;
♀ HB 659–741 mm, T 623–778 mm.
Weight: ♂ 15–26.8 kg; ♀ 11–15.5 kg.
Status: Secure.

Ian Morris

Antilopine Wallaroo
Macropus antilopinus (antelope long-foot)

While this wallaroo prefers flat or undulating country, it sometimes shares rocky habitats with Common and Black Wallaroos. Lives in groups of up to 8, but may form mobs of 30 when threatened.

Habitat: Tropical woodland with grass understorey. **Behaviour:** Terrestrial, gregarious, active from late afternoon. **Diet:** Grass, ground plants, shrubs. **Breeding:** All year, peaking at end of wet season. Gestation about 34 days, pouch life of approximately 9 months. **Features:** Fur is reddish tan above with paler underbelly and limbs. Females can be all or partly grey. Paws and tips of feet are

black. **Length:** ♂ HB 965–1200 mm, T 780–890 mm; ♀ HB 778–835 mm, T 679–700 mm. **Weight:** ♂ 30–49 kg; ♀ 16–20 kg. **Status:** Secure.

Black Wallaroo
Macropus bernardus (Bernard's long-foot)

This is the smallest and most timid of the wallaroos, and is found on the Arnhem Land escarpment and plateau. During the day it rests in the shade, but may be active on overcast days.

Habitat: Monsoon forest, woodland with sparse grass and shrubs. **Behaviour:** Terrestrial, mostly solitary, mainly nocturnal. **Diet:** Grass, ground plants, shrubs. **Breeding:** Relatively unknown, possibly peaks late in summer.
Features: Males are sooty brown to black, females pale grey to grey-brown. Both have dark paws, feet and tail-tips. Ears are relatively short.

Length: ♂ HB 595–725 mm, T 545–640 mm; ♀ avg 646 mm, T avg 575 mm. **Weight:** ♂ 19–22 kg; ♀ avg 13 kg. **Status:** Secure.

Common Wallaroo
Macropus robustus (robust long-foot)

This large, stocky macropod can be found on escarpments and rocky slopes throughout most of Australia. West of the Great Dividing Range it is known as the Euro.

Habitat: Eucalypt forest, woodland, shrubland, grassland.
Behaviour: Terrestrial, mostly solitary, active from early evening.
Diet: Grass, ground plants, shrubs.
Breeding: All year, 1 young. Gestation of 34 days, pouch life of 261 days in east, 244 days in west. Matures at 18 to 24 months.
Features: Eastern animals have coarse, shaggy, dark grey fur. Western animals have shorter reddish fur, although young males may be grey. Both types of females may be bluish grey. All have a large, black, furless nose.
Length: ♂ HT 1138–1986 mm, T 551–901 mm; ♀ HT 1107–1580 mm, T 534–749 mm.
Weight: ♂ 7.25–46.5 kg; ♀ 6.25–25 kg.
Status: Secure.

Western Grey Kangaroo
Macropus fuliginosus (sooty long-foot)

The Western Grey is found in semi-arid habitats across southern Australia west of the Great Dividing Range. The males, also known as Stinkers, have a strong odour and are particularly aggressive.

Habitat: Woodland, shrubland.
Behaviour: Terrestrial, gregarious, active late afternoon to early morning. **Diet:** Grass, broad-leaved ground plants, sometimes shrubs. **Breeding:** All year with summer peak. Gestation 30.5 days, pouch life of 42 weeks. Females sexually active by 20 months, males at 2.5 to 4 years.
Features: Light to chocolate brown flecked with grey. Paws, feet and tail-tip can be darker. Finely furred snout with hairs between upper lip and nostrils.

Length: ♂ HB 521–1225 mm, T 425–1000 mm; ♀ HB 528–931 mm, T 443–815 mm. **Weight:** ♂ 3–53.5 kg; ♀ 4.5–27.5 kg. **Status:** Secure.

Eastern Grey Kangaroo
Macropus giganteus (gigantic long-foot)

The Eastern Grey is found on coastal plains, the Great Dividing Range and inland plains where annual rainfall exceeds 250 mm. In mobs, males and females have separate hierarchies.

Habitat: Forest, woodland, shrubland.
Behaviour: Terrestrial, gregarious, active late afternoon to early morning.
Diet: Grass, broad-leaved ground plants, sometimes shrubs.
Breeding: All year with summer peak. Gestation of 36 days, pouch life about 44 weeks, weaned by 18 months. Females sexually active by 20 months, males at 2.5 to 4 years.
Features: Light to dark grey above, ends of paws, feet and tail can be darker grey to black. Females usually have white chest. Finely furred snout with hairs between upper lip and nostrils.

Length: ♂ HB 542–1212 mm, T 430–1090 mm; ♀ HB 512–1015 mm, T 446–842 mm. **Weight:** ♂ 4–66 kg; ♀ 3.5–32 kg. **Status:** Secure.

Red Kangaroo *Macropus rufus* (red long-foot)

The Red Kangaroo can be found over most of central and western Australia where annual rainfall is less than 500 millimetres. It may live in an extended family group or in mobs numbering several hundred.

Habitat: Open woodland, grassland, desert.
Behaviour: Terrestrial, gregarious, semi-nomadic, most active from late afternoon to early morning.
Diet: Grass, broad-leaved ground plants, sometimes shrubs.
Breeding: All year. Gestation of 33 days, pouch life of 34 weeks. Mature at 2 to 3 years.
Lifespan: Up to 20 years.
Features: Short dense fur. Eastern males usually rusty red and females blue-grey. In western regions, both sexes are red. Whitish belly, chest and limbs. Squarish snout with distinctive black and white patches around the nose. Broad white cheek stripe.
Length: ♂ HB 935–1400 mm, T 710–1000 mm; ♀ HB 745–1100 mm, T 645–900 mm.
Weight: ♂ 22–85 kg; ♀ 17–35 kg.
Status: Secure.

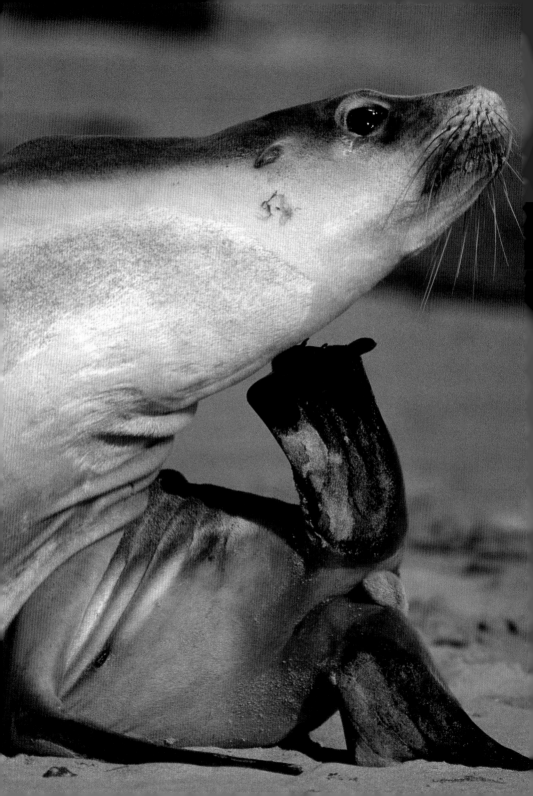

PLACENTALS

There are more kinds and greater numbers of eutherian, or placental, mammals in the world than there are marsupial and monotreme mammals. They successfully exploit the Earth's terrestrial resources as well as its marine habitats. While their method of reproduction is no more efficient than a marsupial's, having a more complex brain structure is a distinct advantage in the competition for survival.

Primitive marine mammals that originated in the northern hemisphere began appearing in Australia's coastal seas about 28 million years ago. Among their descendants that now breed here, or are regular visitors, are several species of seals, dolphins, whales and the Dugong.

Bats were the first terrestrial placental mammals to migrate to Australia, arriving some 55 million years ago just prior to the final break up of Gondwana. They were followed by the first rodents that crossed the narrowing gap between Australia and South-East Asia about four to five million years ago. Bats and rodents now represent about 46% of all native mammal species in Australia.

Rising sea levels delayed the arrival of other placental mammals until the human species discovered sea travel. Their successful colonisation of Australia was assisted by the other placental mammals they brought with them. Although many of these introduced species are widespread and well established, they are not considered native mammals.

Above: Dingos.
Left: Australian Sea-lion.

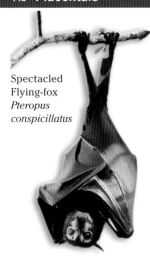

Spectacled
Flying-fox
*Pteropus
conspicillatus*

Bats

Bats are the only mammals that are able to fly, thanks to thin sheets of skin supported by modified arms and extremely long fingers. These winged placental mammals belong to the order **Chiroptera**, meaning "winged hand". They are divided into two suborders commonly known as megabats and microbats. Almost 80 species of bats live in Australia and they represent about 20% of its native mammalian fauna. In keeping with their tropical origins, most are found in warm humid environments. Two-thirds of Australia's bat species occur on Cape York in Queensland compared with only eight species in Tasmania.

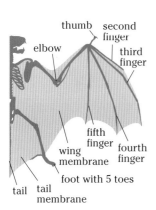

thumb   second
          finger

elbow   third
              finger

fifth
finger   fourth
wing   finger
membrane

foot with 5 toes

tail tail
      membrane

A Grey-headed Flying Fox.

✗ Australia's 12 species of megabats include flying-foxes, blossom-bats and tube-nosed bats.

✗ Megabats play an important role in the pollination of trees and the distribution of their seeds.

✗ Male flying-foxes scent their necks to attract females. Each species has a characteristic odour.

Megabats

Megabats (suborder **Megachiroptera**) eat fruit, flowers or nectar. They find food by sight, smell and the noise of other bats feeding. They have claws on their first and second fingers. The tail is short or nonexistent. They hang upside down to rest and wrap their wings around the body like a cloak. While most megabats are large, blossom-bats are around 60 millimetres in length.

Learning to Fly

A flying-fox cannot fly when it is born and is carried by its mother for the first month or so. It clings to her with its claws and curved milk teeth and feeds on demand from a nipple located near each armpit. When a young one is strong enough to roost, it is left in camp at night. By two months of age it can fly but does not join the nightly fly-out for another month.

Social Structure

Flying-foxes are intelligent, gregarious animals. Daytime roosts or camps are where they court, mate, raise their young, squabble over territories and occasionally sleep. Beneath the chaotic noise of a large camp lies a complex social structure. There may be border guards, food scouts, breeding pairs, separate groups of youths and even nursery trees. Some camps are used for a few weeks; others may be occupied for several months. When local food supplies dwindle, the bats move to another camp. During the breeding season, hundreds of thousands may congregate at a single camp.

A colony of the Black Flying-foxes roosts among the trees at its daytime camp.

✘ A Black Flying-fox travelling at 40 km/h beats its wings about 120 times per minute.

✘ Megabats do not use echolocation to navigate or find food.

✘ A blossom-bat collects nectar with its bristly tongue and eats pollen groomed from its fur.

Finding Megabats

Flying-fox camps are located easily by the noise and smell, and by spectacular mass fly-outs at dusk.

At night listen for the chatter and flapping wings of individuals in fig, palm, mango and other fruiting trees.

Coastal heath with banksias are good spots to look for night-feeding blossom-bats and tube-nosed bats.

Flying-foxes can be carriers of viruses harmful to humans and should not be handled.

Location Tips

→ Brisbane, Qld
→ Daintree NP, Qld
→ Kakadu NP, NT
→ Ballina, NSW
→ Melbourne, Vic

Ghost Bat
Macroderma gigas

✘ The carnivorous Ghost Bat, with a wingspan of up to 600 mm, is the world's largest microbat.

✘ During their annual migration, bent-wing bats may fly more than 1,000 km.

✘ Many microbats have elaborate ear and nose structures for transmitting and receiving ultrasonic frequencies.

✘ A microbat can eat up to 50% of its own body weight in insects each night.

✘ Microbats roost in caves, tree hollows, crevices, culverts, abandoned mines, buildings, tunnels, under bark and even in curled leaves.

✘ Two species of microbats are endangered and three species are listed as vulnerable.

Microbats

Microbats (suborder **Microchiroptera**) have only one claw on the leading edge of each wing and usually rest with their wings folded against the body. Most have small eyes. They live alone or in groups and use a variety of hidden sites as daytime roosts. Microbats are nocturnal predators that hunt and navigate by sight and echolocation.

High Frequency Transmitters

Each type of microbat has its own set of echolocation signals that suits its habitat and the way it catches food. A bat's larynx generates sound pulses ranging from 5 to 200 kHz. These are sent out through the mouth and nostrils. Pulses that bounce back off surrounding objects are picked up by the bat's large ears. These sound echoes can tell a bat the size and location of its prey, how fast it is moving and in what direction.

The Ghost Bat is one of the largest microbats in the world and the largest in Australia.

Hibernation

Microbats need a lot of energy to fly and to replace body heat lost through their large wing surfaces. During winter they have trouble finding enough insects to meet these high energy requirements. While some species migrate, others hibernate until conditions improve. When a bat shuts down operations, its body temperature drops to 2–3°C above that of its surroundings and it survives on stored body fat. The last of these reserves is used when the bat awakens and has to exercise its wings before being able to fly. Consequently, it can have disastrous effects on a colony of microbats if they are disturbed during hibernation.

A close-up of the Ghost Bat's noseleaf

A long-eared bat, *Nyctophilus* sp. The long-eared bats are members of the large **Vespertilionidae** family.

Finding Microbats

Microbats emerge at dusk to hunt. Look for them:

- zeroing in on insects around house and street lights;
- swooping over the surface of ponds, streams and dams;
- flying along forest walking tracks;
- scrabbling on the forest floor and among shrubs.

Hibernating bats should not be disturbed.

Location Tips

→ Tunnel Creek NP, WA
→ Mt Etna NP, Qld
→ Litchfield NP, NT
→ Jenolan Caves, NSW

Ian Morris

Black Flying-fox
Pteropus alecto (Fury wing-foot)

This flying-fox's habitats include mangrove and paperbark swamps as well as rainforest. It roosts high in the canopy and is a noisy feeder. Camps in northern estuaries may hold hundreds of thousands, but smaller camps are more usual.

Habitat: Rainforest, eucalypt forest, mangroves, paperbark swamps.
Breeding: Young are born October to December, but, in the north, young have been recorded all months.
Features: Short black fur often tipped with white. Reddish collar on back of neck. Brown eye-rings may be present. Leg fur extends to knees. Wingspan can be greater than 1 m.

Length: HB 240–260 mm; forearm 150–182 mm.
Weight: 500–700 g.
Status: Secure.

Spectacled Flying-fox
Pteropus conspicillatus (spectacled wing-foot)

These beguiling bats camp by the thousands in mangroves, paperbark swamps and rainforest. They fly out at dusk in all directions to feed in pairs on eucalypt flowers and rainforest fruit. These bats are thought to be important long-distance dispersal agents for the seeds of rainforest trees.

Habitat: Rainforest, mangroves, paperbark swamps.
Breeding: A single young is born between October and December. Juveniles are nursed for 5 months or more.
Features: Dark brown to black, sometimes grey flecked. Yellowish fur surrounds eyes and extends to snout. Yellow-orange neck ruff; silvery in some bats. Legs furred to knees.
Length: HB 220–240 mm; forearm ♂ 160–180 mm, ♀ 155–175 mm
Weight: ♂ 580–850 g; ♀ 500–650 g.
Status: Vulnerable.

Grey-headed Flying-fox
Pteropus poliocephalus (grey-headed wing-foot)

This mainly coastal species roosts in forest and
mangrove trees. It feeds in groups of up to 10 on
fruit (sometimes farmed fruit) and blossoms. Camps
are often located near water in gullies with dense
vegetation. Large summer breeding camps are shared
with Little Red and Black Flying-foxes.

Habitat: Rainforest, eucalypt forest, swamps.
Breeding: Most young are born in October; a few are
born as late as February.
Features: Dark brown shaggy fur. Grey head and
underside. Reddish yellow mantle surrounds neck. Leg
fur extends to ankles. Wingspan can
exceed 1 m.
Length: HB 230–289 mm;
forearm 138–180 mm.
Weight: 600–1000 g
Status: Vulnerable.

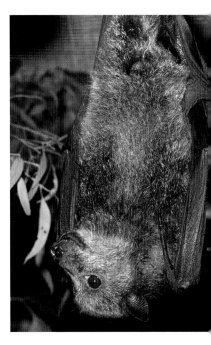

Little Red Flying-fox
Pteropus scapulatus (notably shouldered wing-foot)

This is the most widespread species of flying-fox and is
found in all States except Tasmania. It supplements its
diet of eucalypt flowers with fruit, leaves, bark, sap and
insects. These nomads form large temporary camps in
forests, woodlands and mangroves. They spiral up from
the canopy and fly out in orderly columns at dusk.

Habitat: Forest, woodland, mangroves.
Breeding: One young is born each year between April
and June.
Features: Reddish brown with light brown to yellow on
neck, shoulders and around eyes. Upper surface of leg
is furless. Reddish brown wings, translucent in flight.
Wingspan is less than 1 m.
Length: HB 195–235 mm;
forearm ♂ 125–156 mm, ♀ 125–148 mm.
Weight: ♂ 350–604 g; ♀ 310–560 g.
Status: Secure.

Klaus Uhlenhut, ANTPhoto.com

Eastern Tube-nosed Bat *Nyctimene robinsoni* (Robinson's moonlight[-bat])

This well-camouflaged bat roosts alone in dense vegetation and feeds, sometimes in small groups, on fruit and blossoms. It often flies along forest pathways close to the ground and has a high-pitched whistling call.

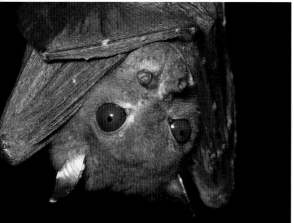

Habitat: Rainforest, eucalypt forest, woodland and heath.
Breeding: Females give birth to 1 young, usually October–December.
Features: Fur is grey to light brown with dark stripe down back. Brown wings. Light green to yellow spots on wings, ears and nostrils. Prominent tubular nostrils. Short tail.
Length: HB 100–110 mm, T 20–25 mm; forearm 60–70 mm.
Weight: 30–50 g.
Status: Secure.

Stan Breeden

Common Blossom-bat
Syconycteris australis (southern fig-bat)

This tiny megabat roosts alone in dense vegetation. It gathers nectar with a long bristly tongue and eats pollen that sticks to its fur. It usually flies 3–5 m above the ground.

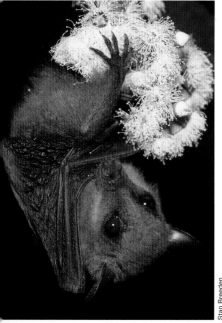

Stan Breeden

Habitat: Rainforest, eucalypt forest, heathland and paperbark swamp.
Breeding: In NSW, 1 young is born October to November and a second February to April. Breeds all year in the north of its range. **Features:** Long, soft fur is fawn to reddish brown and extends to ankles. Paler, sometimes white flecked below. Slender pointed snout. No tail. Large first claw on wing.
Length: HB 40–60 mm; forearm 38–45 mm.
Weight: ♂ 16–22 g; ♀ 16–26 g.
Status: Secure.

Ghost Bat *Macroderma gigas*
(giant large-skin)

Australia's largest microbat eats insects, frogs, reptiles, birds and small mammals, mostly caught on the ground then taken to feeding sites. It roosts in caves, crevices and mines.

Habitat: Scattered throughout north.
Breeding: Single young, September to November. **Features:** Soft fur is light to dark grey above, pale grey to white below. Long ears joined at centre of forehead. Simple nose leaf. Large eyes. No tail.
Length: HB 100–130 mm; forearm 102–112 mm.
Weight: 140–165 g.
Status: Vulnerable.

Diadem Leafnosed-bat
Hipposideros diadema (diadem horseshoe [-bat])

This species uses a variety of daytime roosts including caves, mines, sheds and tree hollows. It hangs from a branch waiting to ambush insects; it returns to the ambush site to eat.

Habitat: Rainforest, eucalypt forest.
Breeding: Females form maternity groups towards the end of the year; single young is born in early summer.
Features: Usually grey to yellowish-brown with pale blotches on shoulders and belly. Dark wings and reddish limbs. Upper part of noseleaf has scalloped edge. Tiny eyes. Pointed ears with horizontal ridges and furred base.
Length: HB 75–85 mm, T 30–40 mm; forearm 78–82 mm.
Weight: 30–50 g.
Status: Secure.

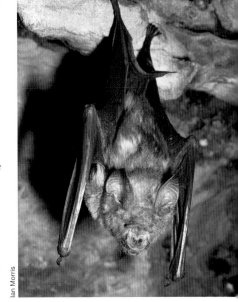

Ian Morris

Ian Morris

Orange Leafnosed-bat
Rhinonicteris aurantius (golden nose-bat)

This brightly coloured bat roosts in warm, humid caves in groups of 20 to several thousand. It changes caves seasonally. It emerges at dusk to hunt for moths, beetles and other insects, returning to its cave several times a night to groom and digest its food.

Habitat: Open woodland.
Breeding: May be seasonal.
Features: Orange fur, sometimes with brown and yellow tinges. Dark brown wings and reddish limbs. Pointed ears. Lower part of noseleaf is broad with centre gap; upper part has scalloped edge. Deep-set nostrils are separated by high ridge.

Length: HB 45–53 mm, T 24–28 mm; forearm 47–50 mm.
Weight: 8–10 g.
Status: Secure.

Jiri Lochman, Lochman Transparencies

Common Sheathtail-bat
Taphozous georgianus
([King] George [Sound] tomb-dweller)

The Common Sheathtail roosts in caves, crevices and old mines. It clings to the rock wall rather than hanging from the roof. It flies in a zigzag or grid pattern when hunting, and feeds in flight.

Habitat: Rocky country of northern Australia.
Breeding: Single, well-developed young, most born in December. Birth weight is up to 25% of the mother's weight.
Features: Dark brown above, lighter below. Yellow-brown hairs underside of tail. Tail protrudes above sliding membrane. Long narrow wings. Nostrils at end of pointed snout. Ridged ears.
Length: HB 75–89 mm, T 21–32 mm; forearm 66–74 mm.
Weight: 19–51 g.
Status: Secure.

Large-footed Myotis
Myotis macropus
(large-footed mouse-ear)

Groups roost in caves, mines, tunnels, buildings, trees. Often seen flying over ponds, lakes and streams, dipping down to catch aquatic insects.

Habitat: Close to bodies of water.
Breeding: In south, breed once a year, twice in central parts, thrice in tropics.
Features: Grey-brown above; paler below. Old bats can be ginger. Large feet and long ankles. Tail enclosed in membrane. Nose overhangs bottom lip.
Length: HB 52–56 mm,
T 36–40 mm;
forearm 38–41 mm.
Weight: 7–12 g.
Status: Secure.

Ian Morris

Hoary Wattled Bat
Chalinolobus nigrogriseus
(black-grey bridle-lobe)

This is usually the first species of microbat to appear at dusk. It catches insects in the air, on the ground and on tree trunks. The Hoary Wattled Bat has a twisting and turning flight. It roosts in tree hollows and rock crevices.

Habitat: Forest, woodland and shrubland.
Breeding: Single young born between September and November.
Features: Blackish grey above with white-tipped hairs. Short head with rounded forehead. Tail enclosed by membrane.
Length: HB 45–55 mm,
T 35–42 mm;
forearm 32–38 mm.
Weight: 7.5–10 g.
Status: Secure.

Ian Morris

Spinifex Hopping-mouse
Notomys alexis

✗ Since European settlement, seven species of native rodents have become extinct, five are endangered and nine species are listed as vulnerable.

✗ The New Holland Mouse was lost for over 120 years and rediscovered near Sydney in 1967.

✗ The Water-rat is one of the few animals able to eat parts of the poisonous Cane Toad.

✗ The Long-tailed Mouse of Tasmania's Antarctic Beech forests mates for life.

✗ Pebble-mound mice carry 5 g stones in their mouths and carefully arrange them around burrow entrances with their front paws.

✗ The Giant White-tailed Rat from north Queensland's tropical forests has been known to open tin cans with its incisor teeth.

Rodents

Mouse-like placental mammals carried from South-East Asia by the sea's flotsam and jetsam first arrived in Australia between 4 and 5 million years ago. Making the most of what their new home had to offer, they spread out, diversified and became uniquely Australian. Two more waves of rodents reached Australian shores during the last two million years and have since become naturalised. The 70 or so species of Australian rats and mice belong to the family **Muridae**. They represent about one quarter of all our native mammal species and can be found in almost every terrestrial habitat.

Diet and Dentition

Rodents are basically herbivores, but readily include insects in their diet when plant food becomes scarce. A rodent has an upper and lower pair of curved, chisel-edged front teeth that grow continuously. Gnawing on tough plants keeps these incisors to a manageable length. They also have three pairs of upper and lower molars, and most lack canine and premolar teeth. Like other herbivores, a rodent has a specialised gut system to break down cellulose and absorb nutrients.

Ian Morris

The Dusky Rat is descended from one of the more recent waves of rodent migrants.

Feast and Famine

Rodents are an important source of food for carnivorous mammals, reptiles and birds. When, following good rains, Australia's dry countryside is carpeted with new plant growth, well-fed rodents breed quickly, often, and in large numbers. These population explosions attract a host of predators that also feed up and breed up quickly.

As the land browns off and rodent numbers drop, most of the carnivores face starvation or migration. A nucleus of predators and prey will survive the dry period that follows, ready to feast and multiply during the next wet season.

Native rodent species and populations have declined since Europeans arrived, probably affected by habitat degradation, introduced predators and increased competition for food.

Peter Slater

A Letter-winged Kite feeds its chicks a Long-haired Rat.

Finding Rodents

Location Tips

Look for tracks with obvious claw marks left by the 4 clawed front toes and 5 clawed hind toes. Check for relatively small, cylindrical scats pointed at one or both ends on runways and at burrow entrances. Some species leave excavated debris at entrances. Try spotlighting tree-rats in the canopies of tropical forests and woodlands.

Found all over Australia in habitats where suitable food and shelter are available.

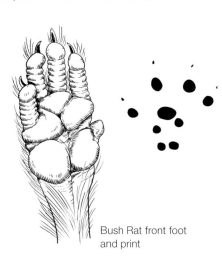

Bush Rat front foot and print

Bush Rat hind foot and print

Hopping-mice have extra-long hind feet and water-rats have partially webbed hind feet.

Brush-tailed Tree-rat *Conilurus penicillatus* (brush[-tailed] rabbit-tail)

This large and vocal rodent lives in northern Australia in family groups that shelter in logs, tree hollows and amongst Pandanus fronds. It is sometimes found in bulky grass nests at the base of trees.

Habitat: Monsoonal north in open eucalypt forest, woodland with grass or shrub under-storey, also coastal stands of Casuarina and Pandanus. **Behaviour:** Terrestrial and arboreal, gregarious, mostly nocturnal. **Diet:** Grass, seeds, insects.

Breeding: March to October. Gestation of 36 days, 48 days when lactating. 1–4 young per litter. Several litters per season. Weaned at 3–7 weeks. **Features:** Grey-brown above with rufous neck patch. Cream to white below, sometimes with grey chest patch. Darker tail ends in black or white brush. White feet. Large ears.

Length: HB 135–227 mm, T 102–235 mm.
Weight: ♂ 116–242 g; ♀ 102–202 g.
Status: Secure.

Ian Morris

Water-rat *Hydromys chrysogaster* (golden-bellied water-rat)

This amphibious rodent is active day and night. It shelters ashore in burrows or hollow logs. It hunts on land and under water. Prey are consumed at established feeding sites on land.

Habitat: Near permanent bodies of fresh or brackish water; sometimes on the seashore. **Behaviour:** Amphibious, active day and night. **Diet:** Aquatic insects, crustaceans, mussels, fish, frogs, lizards, waterbirds, small mammals. **Breeding:** All year with a spring–summer peak. Gestation of 34 days, 3–4 young, up to 5 litters a year. Females may mature at 4 months, usually 8 months.

Features: Sleek, thick, waterproof fur is black to grey or brown above, white to orange below. Moults twice a year. Thick tail with white tip. Small ears. Broad, partially webbed hind feet.

Length: ♂ HB 231–345 mm, T 227–320 mm; ♀ HB 245–370 mm, T 242–325 mm.
Weight: ♂ 400–1275 g; ♀ 340–992 g.
Status: Secure.

Ian Morris

Greater Stick-nest Rat *Leporillus conditor* (builder little-hare)

Once common in semi-arid regions of southern Australia, the species now occurs naturally only on Franklin Island in the Great Australian Bight. This stick-nest rat uses branches to build large, communal nests lined with grass and leaves, housing up to 20 individuals.

Habitat: Open woodland and shrubland.
Behaviour: Terrestrial, gregarious, mostly nocturnal.
Diet: Leaves and fruit or succulent plants such as Pigface.

Breeding: All year with an autumn–winter peak. Gestation of 30 days; 1–3 young are weaned at 1 month.
Features: Fluffy fur is yellowish brown to grey above, creamy white below. White markings on hind feet. Large ears and rounded snout. Furred tail is dark brown above and light brown underneath.
Length: HB 170–260 mm, T 145–180 mm.
Weight: 180–450 g.
Status: Endangered.

Grassland Melomys *Melomys burtoni* (Burton's Melanesian-mouse)

This common rodent is an agile climber and usually builds a spherical nest above the ground. Most nests have two entrances.

Habitat: Coastal grassland, forests, woodland, swamps, mangroves, canefields.
Behaviour: Terrestrial and arboreal.
Diet: Seeds, fruit, plant stems, insects.
Breeding: All year (WA, NT), seasonal (Qld).
Features: Varies from dark grey through grey-brown to reddish brown above, paler below. Sometimes pale orange on sides. Mosaic pattern of scales on sparsely furred, semi-prehensile tail.

Length: ♂ HB 90–160 mm, T 90–175 mm; ♀ HB 95–145 mm, T 100–170 mm.
Weight: ♂ 26–124 g; ♀ 26–97 g.
Status: Secure.

Ian Morris

Spinifex Hopping-mouse *Notomys alexis* (Alexandria Downs southern mouse)

This unusual rodent is found on sand flats and dunes in the arid regions of central and western Australia. It shelters from the desert heat in metre-deep burrow systems that have several vertical entrances. The population increases very quickly after good rain, sinking back to a lower level as conditions dry.

Habitat: Woodland, grassland and desert with spinifex hummocks.

Behaviour: Terrestrial, nocturnal. **Diet:** Seeds, roots, leaf shoots, insects. **Breeding:** All year with spring peak. Normal gestation of 32 days, when 1–6 young are born. Mature at 2 months.
Features: Light brown above, grey-white below. Long, tufted tail. Long hind feet and legs, upright stance. Large, rounded, sparsely furred ears. Bare chest patch.

Length: HB 95–112 mm, T 131–150 mm.
Weight: 27–45 g.
Status: Secure.

Ash-grey Mouse *Pseudomys albocinereus* (white-grey false-mouse)

The Ash-grey Mouse is found in Western Australia in semi-arid habitats from Cape Arid National Park to islands in Shark Bay. It prefers sandy soils where family groups live in complex burrow systems up to 600 mm deep and 3–4 metres in length. For most of the year the Ash-grey Mouse does not need to drink water; it gets sufficient moisture from its food.

Jiri Lochman, Lochman Transparencies

Habitat: Heath, mallee shrubland.
Behaviour: Terrestrial, gregarious, nocturnal.
Diet: Seeds, other plant material, small arthropods. **Breeding:** Spring, 38 days gestation. 2–6 young are mature by August.
Features: Long, soft fur is silver-grey tinged with fawn above, white below. Pink paws. Large rounded ears.
Length: ♂ HB 63–95 mm, T 95–105 mm;
♀ HB 63–85 mm, T 85–97 mm.
Weight: ♂ 30–40 g;
♀ 14–29 g.
Status: Secure.

Plains Rat *Pseudomys australis* (southern false-mouse)

The Plains Rat is restricted to the Lake Eyre basin and the Nullarbor Plain near the SA–WA border. It lives in underground colonies that are connected by surface runways. The Plains Rat lacks sweat glands, which helps it to survive without drinking.

Habitat: Arid shrubland and gibber plains.
Behaviour: Terrestrial, gregarious, nocturnal.
Diet: Seeds, other plant material, insects.
Breeding: Usually after heavy rain. Gestation of 30–31 days, 1–7 young (normally 3–4) that are weaned at 28 days.
Features: Grey to grey-brown above, white or cream below. Relatively large ears. Tail is lighter towards the tip and is less than or equal to the length of the head and body.
Length: HB 100–140 mm, T 80–120 mm.
Weight: 50–80 g.
Status: Vulnerable.

Kakadu Pebble-mound Mouse *Pseudomys calabyi* (Calaby's false-mouse)

This rodent was discovered in 1973 and so far has only been found in the South Alligator River catchment. It surrounds its tunnel entrances with piles of small stones that are used to block access for predators, such as the Western Brown Snake. Because it is known from such a limited area, great care has been taken with this species' conservation.

Habitat: Grassy woodland on gravel soils.
Behaviour: Terrestrial, mostly nocturnal.
Diet: Seeds, other plant material.
Breeding: Little is known, but, in captivity, all year, with up to 7 litters per year.
Features: Grey-brown above, pale orange sides, white below. Pointed snout. Large protruding eyes. The tail is shorter than the head and body.
Length: ♂ HB 69–95 mm, T 72–94 mm; ♀ HB 68–82 mm, T 64–85 mm.
Weight: ♂ 15–31 g; ♀ 12–23 g.
Status: Secure.

Ian Morris

Delicate Mouse *Pseudomys delicatulus* (delicate false-mouse)

This small rodent prefers the open, sparsely vegetated habitats that are found across tropical northern Australia. During the day it shelters from the sun's heat in shallow burrows, termite mounds and hollow logs.

Habitat: Open woodland, grassland, coastal dunes. **Behaviour:** Terrestial, nocturnal.
Diet: Mostly native grass seeds. **Breeding:** All year in favourable conditions. Gestation of

Ian Morris

28–31 days, usually 3–4 young per litter and several litters per year. Weaned by 1 month old.
Features: Yellow-brown to grey-brown above, white or cream below. Nose and feet are pale pink. Long, slender tail.

Length: HB 55–75 mm, T 55–80 mm.
Weight: 6–15 g.
Status: Secure.

Bush Rat *Rattus fuscipes* (dusky-footed rat)

Michael Morcombe

The Bush Rat prefers habitats with dense undergrowth and is susceptible to bushfires and logging activities. It shelters during the day in short tunnels dug under logs and rocks.

Habitat: Rainforest, eucalypt forest, woodland.
Behaviour: Terrestrial, mostly solitary, nocturnal.
Diet: Insects, grass, leaves, fungi.
Breeding: All year, 5 young per litter, several litters per year. The young are weaned at 4–5 weeks and are mature at 4 months.
Features: Soft, thick fur is grey-brown to reddish brown above, paler below. Brown, grey or black tail with rings of scales. Tail is shorter than head–body length. Rounded ears. Hind feet are usually darker than front feet.
Length: HB 111–214 mm, T 105–195 mm.
Weight: 40–225 g.
Status: Secure.

Pale Field-rat *Rattus tunneyi* (Tunney's rat)

This attractive rodent favours grassy habitats with sandy soil. It makes shallow burrows with numerous entrances that are marked by small piles of soil and droppings. It also shelters in termite mounds. The Pale Field-rat's preferred habitats near creek banks have been damaged by introduced mammals such as Rabbits, sheep, cattle and goats. It has maintained a stronghold in the north where the landscape has suffered less modification.

Habitat: Grassy woodland, grassland.
Behaviour: Terrestrial, mostly solitary, nocturnal.
Diet: Seeds, roots, grass stems.
Breeding: Spring in the east, January to August in NT and WA. Gestation of 21–22 days, 2–11 young. Weaned at 3 weeks, mature at 5 weeks.
Features: Shiny coat is yellow-brown above, grey or cream below. Scaly tail is shorter than head and body. Large eyes. Female has 10 teats. **Length:** 118–198 mm, T 78–190 mm.
Weight: 42–206 g.
Status: Secure.

Ian Morris

Common Rock-rat *Zyzomys argurus* (silver-tailed zyzomys [meaning unknown])

This is the most widespread of the five species of rock-rats. If the delicate skin on the tail is torn away, the tail withers. An earlier name for these species was "thick-tailed rats", which refers to the animals' most distinctive feature.

Habitat: Rocky outcrops, which provide shelter for nesting, within open forest or woodland with a grassy understorey.
Behaviour: Terrestrial, mostly nocturnal.
Diet: Leaves, stems, seeds, fungi, insects.
Breeding: All year. Gestation of 35 days, 1–4 young that mature at 5–6 months. Young are left in the nest, not carried with the mother.
Features: Light brown above, white below. The sparsely furred tail has a thick base. The tail is often damaged or missing.
Length: HB 85–122 mm, T up to 125 mm.
Weight: 26–55 g.
Status: Secure.

Ian Morris

Dingo

The Dingo is a primitive member of the **Canidae** family and is thought to have evolved from the Indian Wolf. It was introduced to Australia from South-East Asia about 5,000 years ago; however, it is commonly regarded as a native animal because it has been here for so long. Having out-competed the Thylacine, it is now the largest carnivorous land mammal in Australia.

Lifestyle

A Dingo's life begins in late winter or early spring when females give birth. A litter usually consists of from three to seven pups. After a few days of constant care, the pups are left alone in a den for much of the time while the mother rests or hunts. Within two weeks they are being fed regurgitated meat as well as milk. When the pups are big enough to travel, they are taken on kills and gradually introduced to the pack's territory. Aside from hunting and sleeping, Dingos spend time socialising and maintaining their territorial boundaries.

The size of the territory depends on the abundance of food and availability of fresh water. In good habitats the average territory is about 10 km². Habitat quality also determines the size of a pack. While forested areas suit packs of around three, 12 or more may be found in packs in undisturbed arid regions.

✗ Dingos breed only once a year.

✗ Dingos usually mate for life.

✗ Domestic dogs and Dingos may interbreed.

A solitary Dingo in thick undergrowth in a forested area.

Hunting Behaviour

Dingos are patient, intelligent hunters with excellent vision, acute hearing and a keen sense of smell. They usually hunt alone, but a pack will work together to bring down large prey.

These opportunistic predators have wide-ranging tastes that include everything from insects to kangaroos. Peak hunting times are dawn and dusk when their favoured prey – Rabbits, rodents and macropods – are on the move and distracted by the business of eating and drinking.

Dingos will organise the size of the pack and their strategy according to the kinds of prey they are hunting. They may cover several kilometres each night when foraging.

In coastal areas, Dingos will prowl the seashore in search of dead animals washed up by the tide. Moulting waterbirds that gather in coastal wetlands are another source of easy food for canny Dingos.

✗ In large packs, the dominant female kills the pups of other females who become nursemaids to her litter.

✗ About 80% of all Dingos in eastern Australia are hybrids.

✗ Dingos mark and defend their territories and groups seldom cross boundaries.

✗ The average lifespan of a wild Dingo is 5 to 7 years.

An opportunistic Dingo feeds on a Swamp Wallaby carcass.

Waterholes attract many kinds of animals and are a favourite hunting spot for Dingos.

Dingos and People

Dingos arrived in Australia as live food for Asian seafarers. They were readily adopted by Australian Aborigines as companions, guards against malevolent night-spirits and possibly as protection against the last of Australia's predatory megafauna. They also assisted with flushing out small game. Dingos appear in Aboriginal art, sometimes replacing older images of the Thylacine, and are the subject of numerous stories of cultural importance.

The war between graziers and Dingos that began in the 1800s continues today. Livestock make up less than 2% of a Dingo's diet. However, once blooded, it will kill for the thrill of the chase, and mixed breed wild dogs are very destructive. Underestimating a Dingo's predatory instincts has led to attacks on people. In tourist areas where Dingos are hand-fed, they may lose their fear of humans. They associate people with food and may attack those they perceive as weaker than themselves.

✘ A fence to keep Dingos out of grazing lands stretches nearly 6,000 km from Queensland's Darling Downs to the Great Australian Bight.

✘ During the 1960s, Dingo hunters or "doggers" in the Victorian Alps were paid a bounty of $4 a scalp.

✘ Dingos prey on fish as desert creeks and waterholes dry up.

A Dingo patrols a beach on Fraser Island searching for food.

Dingos are a popular exhibit at zoos and wildlife sanctuaries.

Finding Dingos

Check waterholes, stock watering points and other sources of fresh water at dawn and dusk. Stake out roadkill on inland roads, rubbish dumps and camping grounds for scavenging Dingos. Listen for characteristic howls and yelps at night. Look for bones and feathers outside likely-looking dens. Look for twisted cylinders or sausage shaped scats on prominent rocks and track intersections.

Location Tips

→ Fraser Island, Qld
→ Uluru–Kata Tjuta NP, NT
→ Nadgee Nature Reserve, NSW
→ Lake Eyre, SA
→ Napier Range, WA

front foot and print

hind foot and print

Dingo *Canis lupus dingo* (wolf dog)

The Dingo is found throughout most of mainland Australia. It prefers habitats where forest or woodlands merge with heath or grassland. Use of arid and semi-arid habitats is determined by the availability of fresh water.

Habitat: All mainland terrestrial habitats.
Behaviour: Terrestrial, gregarious (but may hunt alone), mostly nocturnal. **Diet:** Reptiles, birds, mammals, fish, insects, fruit. **Breeding:** April to June. Gestation of 63 days, 1–10 pups, which are weaned at 3–4 months. Females mature at 2 years.
Features: Fur is usually ginger with white chest, paws and tail-tip. About 4% are black with tan points. Completely white Dingos are sometimes seen in arid habitats. Brindling and colour patches indicate crossbreeds. Bushy tail. Upright ears. Skull is larger, snout narrower and teeth larger than in a domestic dog.
Length: HB 860–1220 mm, T 260–380 mm.
Weight: 9.6–24 kg.
Status: Secure.

Male Australian Sea-lion
Neophoca cinerea

Seals

Seals are thought to have originated in the north Atlantic region with the **Otariidae** family of eared seals appearing about 23 million years ago, getting a headstart on the **Phocidae** (earless seals) that appeared about 15 million years ago. Fossils from south-east Victoria indicate that earless seals were resident Australians about five million years ago and that their eared counterparts made it this far south three million years later.

Seals are amphibious carnivores that have held on to the fur coat, four-limbed body plan and ability to move on land inherited from their terrestrial ancestors. However, feet were exchanged for flippers and their bodies were streamlined in a successful bid to exploit the world's temperate and polar marine environments. Despite their aquatic adaptations, seals are still tied to the land, for this is where they give birth.

✘ Seal hunting was legal in Tasmania until 1923.

✘ Eared seals have 34 or 36 teeth.

✘ A seal's blood can carry three times more oxygen than human blood.

✘ A female Australian Sea-lion has an 18-month breeding cycle.

✘ The Australian Fur-seal can dive to 130 m.

✘ Eared seals seldom stay underwater for more than 5 minutes.

✘ Male New Zealand Fur-seals do not feed during the breeding season, which can last over 2 months.

Movement in Water

These air-breathing mammals may be ungainly on land, but they move through the water with surprising speed and grace thanks to a flexible skeleton, power-packed muscles and flippered limbs. Eared seals row with their large front flippers; earless seals use alternate kicks of the hind flippers.

Before diving, a seal pumps up its oxygen supply with some deep breathing and slows its heart rate. It then closes its nostrils and soft palate to prevent water from entering the lungs and gullet. A layer of fatty blubber beneath the skin and a sleek, double-layered coat of hair streamline and insulate the body.

Large colonies of New Zealand Fur-seals breed on southern rocky coasts and offshore islands.

Seals of Australian Waters

The Australian Sea-lion, New Zealand Fur-seal and Australian Fur-seal breed on the coast of the southern Australian mainland, Tasmania and offshore islands. Other species occasionally visit Tasmanian beaches. The places where seals come ashore to rest are called "haul-out sites".

These accomplished underwater hunters seek out prey by sight, sound and smell. Eared seals have the added advantage of rotatable whiskers that help locate small prey on the sea floor. Their seafood diet includes squid, octopus, fish, crustaceans and penguins. Some eat the pups of other species. When foraging, seals may travel vast distances and swim to great depths.

Seals were hunted in the last century for their meat, oil and fur. Today, all seals are protected in Australia.

The sleek Australian Sea-lion comes to shore to rest and breed.

Australian Fur-seals are the largest and most common fur-seals found in Australia.

✗ Elephant seals can dive to 1,200 m and remain submerged for more than an hour.

✗ The Leopard Seal preys on penguins and the young of other seals.

✗ Some species of earless seals sleep and mate under water.

✗ Female fur-seals can delay the development of their fertilised eggs.

✗ Male Australian Fur-seals live up to 19 years; females up to 21 years.

Location Tips

→ Montague Island, NSW
→ Phillip Island, Vic
→ Cape Bridgewater, Vic
→ Kangaroo Island, SA
→ Eyre Peninsula, SA
→ Head of Bight, SA
→ Seal Island, WA
→ Archipelago of the Recherche, WA
→ Leeuwin–Naturaliste NP, WA
→ Bridport, Tas
→ Bruny Island, Tas

Boat Tours

→ Phillip Island, Vic
→ Esperance, WA
→ Stanley, Tas

Boat excursions offer a close-up look at seal colonies.

Coming Ashore to Rest and Breed

Australia's southern shores and islands host substantial populations of fur-seals and sea-lions. They are more terrestrial than their earless relatives and can turn their hind limbs forward to walk in a semi-upright position. Sea-lions haul out on sandy beaches to rest and moult while fur-seals prefer rocky shores. They all favour rocky sites for mating and raising their young. The arrival of mature males at the rookeries signals the start of the breeding season. While pregnant females are staking out their birthing sites, the males aggressively challenge one another for mating territories and success is directly related to size.

Males may be sexually mature by the age of four, but are seldom big enough to claim a territory until eight or nine years of age. A female gives birth to a single pup conceived during the previous season before she accepts the advances of a dominant male. She develops a strong bond with her pup through touch, smell and calls, allowing quick recognition amidst the chaos of a large colony. The pup is left in a safe crevice or nursery while its mother goes off to feed. It begins accompanying its mother on fishing expeditions at about eight months of age and is usually weaned by the start of the next breeding season.

A female Australian Sea-lion establishes a strong bond with her pup until after it is weaned.

Long sensitive whiskers help eared seals locate food under water.

Curious Australian Fur-seals approach a diver.

Watching Seals

Summer, when they gather in large breeding colonies, is the best time to see fur-seals and sea-lions. Just remember they are very territorial and aggressive at this time and should not be approached.

Seal watchers can take advantage of viewing platforms at various locations along the coast or take a boat tour to offshore haul-out and breeding sites. Visitors to Kangaroo Island can take a guided walk amongst basking sea-lions.

Solitary earless seals are more likely to be seen in coastal waters or stranded on the beach during winter.

Divers should be aware that while seals are very approachable under water, they are also a favoured food of large sharks and Killer Whales.

Earless Visitors

Earless seals no longer reside in Australia having been driven from its shores by the fur trade, but they occasionally venture into coastal waters. Their torpedo-shaped bodies have short front flippers and no visible ears. The backward-facing hind flippers are used for swimming but do not support the body on land, so they inch along on their bellies.

Earless Seals

Crab-eater Seal

Leopard Seal

Ross Seal

Southern Elephant Seal

Weddell Seal

Young Southern Elephant Seal

Australian Sea-lion *Neophoca cinerea* (ash-coloured new-seal)

Australia's only endemic seal breeds on islands from Houtman Abrolhos, Western Australia, to Kangaroo Island, South Australia, and on the mainland at Point La Batt, South Australia. The total population is estimated to be between 11,000 and 13,000.

Habitat: Cool temperate seas with sandy and rocky shores. **Breeding:** August to January. Females breed every 18 months. Gestation of 14–15 months, 1 pup per mating. Weaned at over 1 year. Sexually mature at 4–5 years, but males do not mate until they can hold a territory. **Features:** Lacks thick undercoat of fur. Males are blackish to chocolate brown with distinct lighter coloured mane. Females and young are smaller and coloured silver-grey above and cream to yellow below. Blunt snout, long, white whiskers and small rolled ears.

Length: ♂ HT 1.85–2.35 m; ♀ HT 1.55–1.65 m.
Weight: ♂ about 300 kg; ♀ about 80 kg.
Status: Secure.

New Zealand Fur-seal *Arctocephalus forsteri* (Forster's bear-head)

This eared seal prefers protected boulder beaches with dense vegetation and tidal pools for its rookeries. Dominant males establish harems of up to 16 females.

Habitat: Cool temperate seas and rocky shores. **Breeding:** November to January. Gestation of 8 months, 1 pup per season. Weaned by 12 months, sexually mature at 4 to 5 years, but males unable to hold territory until 8 or 9 years. **Features:** Dark brown to greyish brown above — looks black when wet — paler below. Dense fur underlies the coat of guard hairs. Males have a massive neck and thick mane. Newborns are black. Head profile slightly concave. Elongated, pointed snout with long whiskers and black tip. Small ears.
Length: ♂ HT 1.5–2.5 m; ♀ HT 1.0–1.5 m.
Weight: ♂ 120–180 kg; ♀ 35–50 kg.
Status: Secure.

Australian Fur-seal
Arctocephalus pusillus (little bear-head)

This is the most abundant seal in Australia. Its range extends from Tasmania to southern New South Wales. Colonies of up to 1,500 form at permanent breeding sites on nine islands.

Habitat: Cool temperate seas and rocky shores with platforms, boulders, caves and pebble beaches. **Breeding:** November to December. Gestation of 11.75 months, 1 pup per season, which is weaned by 12 months. Females mature at 3–6 years, males at 4–5 years but are unable to hold territory until at least 8 years old. **Features:** Thick undercoat of fur beneath sleek guard hairs. Males are dark brown to brownish grey with a mane of long coarse hair. Females and young are light brown to silver grey and have a fawn to cream throat. Newborns are black. Slightly pointed snout with long whiskers. Small ears.
Length: ♂ HT 2.01–2.27 m; ♀ HT 1.36–1.71 m.
Weight: ♂ 218–360 kg; ♀ 41–113 kg.
Status: Secure.

Watching Dugongs

Look for Dugongs in wide, shallow bays, mangrove channels, estuaries, on the leeward side of large coastal islands and near coral reefs. Check out offshore sheltered locations in rough weather.

Watch for Dugongs feeding inshore on the rising tide. They surface to breathe about once a minute.

Dugongs are inquisitive and will approach divers.

Location Tips

→ Moreton Bay, Qld
→ Hinchinbrook Channel, Qld
→ Shark Bay, WA
→ Van Diemen Gulf, NT

✘ Dugongs usually stay within 5 m of the surface, although they have been seen as deep as 20 m.

✘ Dugongs have been known to stray as far south as Albany, WA, and Tathra, NSW.

Pilot Fish and Remoras accompany a Dugong as it swims.

Dugong

These rotund, bewhiskered mammals and their Manatee relatives are thought to be the reality behind the myth of irresistible south sea nymphs who lured mariners to destruction on rocky coasts. Rather than enchanting sailors with seductive songs, Dugongs cruise Australia's warm coastal waters in pursuit of lush seagrass meadows. Aside from large old males that use whistling sounds to keep their herds together, the Dugong's musical ability is limited to soft chirps.

Dugongs, also known as sea cows, are herbivorous marine mammals that belong to the order **Sirenia**. A heavy skeleton provides the necessary ballast to keep a Dugong on the sea floor as its flexible and sensitive upper lip pushes seagrass into the mouth. If leaves and new shoots are scarce, it ploughs up whole plants, leaving distinctive furrows in the silt.

Seagrass beds are a vital food source for Dugongs.

Ancient Mariners

A Dugong's lifespan can exceed 70 years, making it one of the longest-lived species of marine mammal. Sexual maturity occurs between the ages of nine and 17 years, at which stage an animal is about 2.4 metres in length and weighs around 250 kilograms.

They have an annual breeding season, but females tend to mate only once every three to seven years. Mating is a fairly violent affair in east coast waters where females are pursued and set upon by several males. In the west, the males establish small territories and it is up to the female to choose a mate. At the end of a 13–14 month pregnancy, a female moves into shallow water protected by a sandbar to give birth to her single offspring.

The calf begins feeding on seagrass within a few weeks of birth, but is not weaned for 12 or more months. It gains some protection from predators such as sharks by riding just above its mother's back when it is not suckling.

- ✗ Habitat degradation, fishing nets, boat propellers and hunting are major threats to Dugong survival.
- ✗ A Dugong's large intestine can be 25 m long.
- ✗ Large sharks, crocodiles and Killer Whales prey on Dugongs.
- ✗ A herd can travel up to 25 km a day.
- ✗ Indigenous Australians harvest about 3,000 Dugongs each year.

Dugong *Dugong dugon* (no translation)

The Dugong lives in shallow, warm water from Shark Bay, Western Australia, around the northern coastline to Moreton Bay, Queensland. Animals travel in herds of up to several hundred.

Habitat: Tropical and subtropical coastal waters.
Diet: Seagrass, sometimes algae and marine invertebrates.
Breeding: Winter through summer, depending on geographic location. Gestation 13–14 months, 1 offspring. Sexually mature at 9–17 years. **Features:** Grey to light brown above, pale below. Two nostrils on top of blunt snout, wide mouth on underside. Sensory bristles on edge and inside surface of enlarged upper lip. Clawless paddle-like front flippers, horizontal tail flukes, no hind limbs and no dorsal fin. Males have two upper tusks.
Length: ♂ HT up to 3.15 m;
♀ HT up to 3.31 m.
Weight: Up to 420 kg.
Status: Vulnerable.

Geoff Taylor, Lochman Transparencies

Bottlenose Dolphin
Tursiops truncatus

✘ Baleen whales have two blowholes; toothed whales have only one.

✘ A Killer Whale will use its head as a battering ram to break through 1-m thick ice to catch resting seals.

✘ A Southern Right Whale has about 300 baleen plates on each side of its mouth.

✘ A Bottlenose Dolphin has about 120 teeth.

✘ A Sperm Whale tooth can be 200 mm long and weigh over 1 kg. Its upper teeth lie below the gum line.

✘ A Blue Whale can consume up to 8 t of krill per day.

✘ An individual Southern Right Whale can be identified by the number, size, shape and position of the callosities on its head.

Whales and Dolphins

Whales and dolphins are members of the order **Cetacea**. The world's 10 species of filter-feeding baleen whales belong to the suborder **Mysticeti** and the 70 species of predatory toothed whales belong to the suborder **Odontoceti**.

Baleen whales are amongst the largest animals in the world. They have arched mouths and hundreds of baleen plates that hang from their upper jaws like curtains. Plankton and small crustaceans such as krill and copepods are caught on these bristle-fringed plates when the whale forces water out of the sides of its mouth.

Toothed whales are a varied group of cetaceans that includes dolphins, sperm whales and the Killer Whale. They have straight jaws lined with numerous peg-like teeth. The teeth are used to grasp prey such as fish and squid, which are then swallowed whole.

Bottlenose Dolphins are toothed cetaceans that cooperate, sometimes with humans, to catch fish.

A Lifetime at Sea

Cetaceans are warm-blooded, air-breathing mammals that spend their whole lives at sea. Their flexible, streamlined bodies are designed for speed swimming and deep diving. Powerful up-and-down strokes of the tail flukes propel the body, while the dorsal fin and side flippers assist with steering and balance. A finely tuned nervous system allows constant adjustment of the body to minimise drag. Several species are known for their spectacular breaches and aerial antics, which are thought to be a form of play, but which also help dislodge skin parasites and may have a communication role.

Cetaceans take in air through their blowholes, which they seal off when diving. The gullet and windpipe are separate so that they do not drown when they open their mouths to feed. Neither do they drown when they become unconscious: breathing is controlled by the voluntary nervous system. (However, they must be lifted to the surface before their oxygen supply is depleted.) Other aquatic adaptations include layers of insulating blubber, enormous lungs and a tolerance of high levels of carbon dioxide. Soft, porous bones and collapsible ribs prevent the ribcage being crushed by water pressure during deep dives.

✘ A spinner dolphin can execute seven horizontal spins during a single leap.

✘ The Sperm Whale can dive to depths exceeding 2,000 m and can remain submerged for more than 2 hours.

✘ Southern Right Whales sometimes raise their tails at right angles to the wind and sail through the water.

✘ In July 2005, the Australian Snubfin Dolphin, *Orcaella heinsohni,* was recognised as a new species.

Humpback Whales are well known for their spectacular surface displays.

Bottlenose Dolphins use over 60 different whistling sounds.

✘ A Bottlenose Dolphin can identify an object the size of a tennis ball from a distance of 120 m.

✘ A Sperm Whale's huge head acts as a sound resonator.

✘ Killer Whale pods have individual sound sequences or dialects that reflect their family ties.

✘ Fin Whales broadcast regular loud groans at a low frequency of 20 Hz to maintain contact with widely spread pod members.

Communicating with Sound

Cetaceans use a variety of sounds to communicate with each other. Their calls and non-verbal but noisy surface behaviours convey information about an individual's identity, location and intentions, and are also used to indicate distress and warn of danger. High frequency whistles and vocal squeaks of various pitches are commonly used by toothed cetaceans such as the Bottlenose Dolphin, while the baleen whales have a more extensive vocal repertoire.

The most complex vocalisations of all cetaceans are the haunting songs of migrating male Humpback Whales. From a range of groans, moans, roars, chirps and trills, two to four sounds are selected and are repeated several times to form a phrase, which is then repeated to form a theme. A song consists of seven or eight themes that are sung in a specific order, and can last up to 15 minutes. All the males on a particular migration route sing the same song, even though it may change over time.

Seeing with Sound

Toothed whales and dolphins use echolocation to navigate and to find food in deep or murky water. Air drawn through the blowhole is squeezed through a series of valves in the nasal sac to produce clicking sounds. The clicks are then transmitted as high-frequency sound waves via fatty tissue in the forehead. The sounds that are bounced back by objects in the wave's path are picked up by the lower jaw, transferred to the middle ear and processed by the brain. This highly advanced sonar system provides three-dimensional information about the size, location and relative distance of objects. With it, a cetacean can not only single out an individual fish in a school, but can assess the school's size and direction of movement.

The remains of a stranded whale.

A female Southern Right Whale and her calf in the shallows of the Great Australian Bight.

Migration

Most cetaceans clock up thousands of kilometres during their lifelong search for food and mates. Baleen whales' annual migrations can exceed 16,000 km. In the southern hemisphere, Humpback and Southern Right Whales leave their cold-water feeding grounds in autumn and head north to breed. After giving birth and mating, they return south and spend the summer filling up on huge quantities of krill and plankton.

From June to October, Southern Right Whales calve and nurse their young in the shallows along Australia's southern coasts, while Humpback Whales use the east and west coasts as highways to and from their tropical breeding grounds. Australia is also a summer feeding ground for Blue Whales. They show up along the coast between Portland, South Australia, and Warrnambool, Victoria, to feed on krill that are nourished by a cold-water upwelling from December to May.

Stranding

Mass stranding remains one of the unsolved mysteries of cetacean behaviour. One theory suggests that whales use the Earth's magnetic field to navigate. Since this field is always changing, they may become temporarily confused and mistakenly swim towards land. Species with strong social bonds, such as pilot whales and dolphins, often strand in groups. Being reluctant to desert one another, pod members may follow a sick, exhausted or disoriented member in to shore.

Solitary strandings usually involve sick or dead cetaceans that have been washed ashore. Presumably when a young animal strands, it has become separated from the herd and lost its way through lack of navigational experience.

✘ About 70% of Humpback Whales that migrate along Australia's east coast are males.

✘ A newborn Southern Right Whale weighs about 1 t.

✘ A litre of whale milk contains 200 g of fat and 20 different proteins.

✘ Female baleen whales give birth every 2 to 3 years.

✘ A Blue Whale calf gains 90 kg a day while suckling.

✘ Sperm Whales live up to 60 years.

✘ "Migaloo", an albino Humpback Whale, has been migrating up the east coast since 1991.

✘ Cetaceans are born tail first and must be lifted to the surface for their first breath.

Bottlenose Dolphins at play.

Humpback Whales migrate in small groups.

✗ Whaling was Australia's first primary industry.

✗ Baleen, also known as whalebone, was used in umbrellas, whips and women's corsets.

✗ The first Australian whaling station opened in 1806 on the Derwent River in Tasmania; the last, at Albany, Western Australia, closed in 1978.

✗ When boiled down, a Blue Whale's body yields 75 barrels of oil.

✗ Whale oil was used for heating and lighting, and to make soap, lubricants, crayons, margarine and paint.

✗ A Humpback Whale is estimated to be worth $100,000 to the tourist industry.

Social Interactions

Whales and dolphins are credited with a high level of intelligence that is often reflected in their sophisticated social interactions. There are several species that display a precocious ability to learn. Young Killer Whales learn from their mothers how to beach themselves and squirm back into the water before accompanying the family on raids to snatch basking seals from the shoreline. At Shark Bay, two generations of mothers in a Bottlenose Dolphin family have imparted to their offspring the protective benefits of wearing a sponge on one's sensitive snout while foraging on an abrasive sea floor.

Cetaceans also seem to have an aptitude for coordinated behaviour that involves vocal communication. Killer Whales use a variety of squeaks and moans when working together to encircle prey or herd them into the shallows. Bottlenose Dolphins and Humpback Whales also signal their mates when corralling prey in bubble-nets. One or more individuals will dive under a shoal of krill or fish and swim in a circle blowing bubbles that rise like a cylindrical curtain trapping prey in the middle. They then lunge upwards through the centre of the net, taking in as much food as their mouths can hold.

A cooperative approach can also be useful in threatening situations. Southern Right Whales will face into a circle and lash their tails against attacking sharks or Killer Whales. Male Sperm Whales have been known to issue warning calls and draw attention to themselves with conspicuous surface displays so that their pods can slip silently away.

Geoff Taylor, Lochman Transparencies

Two female Killer Whales, identified by their shorter, hooked dorsal fins, with a male whose dorsal fin is tall and erect.

Common Surface Behaviours

Blow: The explosive exhalation followed by inhalation of air; also the cloud of droplets that forms when a whale breathes out.

Breaching: Launching the body head first out of the water and falling back with a splash. All or part of the body may be exposed.

Fluking: Lifting the tail into the air, often before a deep dive. The flukes (fins) may be raised to show the underside or turned down.

Flipper slapping: Slapping the waving flippers against the surface of the water, often making a very loud noise.

Lobtailing: Raising the tail and slapping the flukes against the surface of the water, sometimes repeatedly.

Spyhopping: Coming vertically out of the water, head first, sometimes turning in a small circle before slipping below the surface.

Location Tips

→ Hervey Bay, Qld
→ North Stradbroke Island, Qld
→ Cape Byron, NSW
→ Cape Howe, NSW
→ Storm Bay, Tas
→ Freycinet NP, Tas
→ Wilsons Promontory, Vic
→ Warrnambool, Vic
→ Portland, SA
→ Coffin Bay NP, SA
→ Head of Bight, SA
→ Cape Leeuwin, WA
→ Broome, WA
→ Shark Bay, WA

Finding Whales and Dolphins

June to October is the best time to look for migrating Humpback and Southern Right Whales. Take a boat tour or visit a prominent headland on a calm, clear day. A good pair of binoculars or a telephoto camera lens is useful for close-up views.

Dolphins are common all year round in coastal waters. They can be seen in shallow bays, wide river mouths and off prominent headlands. Look for them body surfing and swimming parallel to the shore just beyond the breakers. They often bow-ride when investigating boats and have been known to swim with divers. Wild dolphins come inshore to be hand fed at Monkey Mia, WA, and Moreton Island, Qld. They also feed inshore regularly at Bunbury, WA.

To identify a cetacean look for:
• body colour and relative size;
• head shape;
• position and shape of dorsal fin, if present;
• shape and colour of flippers and tail flukes;
• size, shape and frequency of blows;
• surface behaviour.

Be aware that live, stranded dolphins and whales may thrash about and inadvertently injure bystanders.

Dolphins come in to interact with humans at Tangalooma on Moreton Island, Queensland.

Southern Right Whale *Eubalaena australis* (southern good [right] whale)

Southern Right Whales come inshore to rest and nurse their calves. Whalers regarded them as the right whales to hunt because they swam slowly, floated when dead, and produced large amounts of oil and baleen.

Diet: Krill, plankton. **Surface behaviour:** May breach up to 10 times in a row. Flukes raised when diving. Flipper waving and slapping, head stands, lobtailing. Sails with flukes raised at right angle to wind. Rarely strands.
Blow: Wide V-shaped blow with 2 columns up to 5 m long. Left column taller than right.
Features: Black, rotund body with irregular white patches on belly. Large white bumps (callosities) on lower jaw, top of head and above eyes. Distinctly arched mouth. Long, dark grey baleen. No dorsal fin. Large, broad flippers with prominent ridges. The tail base is narrow and the flukes have smooth, concave edges.

Length: 13–18 m.
Weight: 30–80 t.
Status: Endangered.

Humpback Whale *Megaptera novaeangliae* (big-winged new-Englander)

The Humpback is one of the most commonly seen whales in coastal waters from June to October. It is best known for its spectacular surface displays. The Humpback is a slow swimmer and can remain submerged for up to 45 minutes.

Diet: Krill, plankton.
Surface behaviour: Breaching, lobtailing, flipper slapping, flipper waving, spyhopping. Flukes exposed at upright angle. Strandings.
Blow: Wide bushy blow up to 3 m high.
Features: Stout body is dark grey to black above and white below. Flat head and small dorsal fin. Knobby protuberances on head, lower jaw and flippers. Flippers are one-third of body length. Flippers and tail flukes have scalloped edges and undersides have unique black and white patterns. 14–35 throat pleats. Black baleen.

Length: 14–19 m.
Weight: 25–30 t.
Status: Vulnerable.

Dwarf Minke Whale *Balaenoptera acutorostrata* (pointed-beaked winged-whale)

The Dwarf Minke is one of the smallest of the baleen whales and is still hunted commercially. It feeds in coastal waters and sometimes enters rivers.

Diet: Krill, plankton, schooling fish. **Surface behaviour:** 45° breach with dorsal fin visible, 5–8 quick blows before diving. Flukes do not show when diving. Spyhops. May investigate boats. Strands occasionally.
Blow: Low diffuse cloud 2–3 m high. **Features:** Dark bluish grey above and white below. Sometimes has wavy line on side. Narrow triangular head with prominent central ridge. Short, yellow-grey baleen, 50–70 throat pleats. Relatively tall, curved dorsal fin beyond middle of back. Slender, pointed flippers can have white band. Tail flukes dark bluish grey above with pale underside.
Length: 6–8 m. **Weight:** 5–9 t. **Status:** Secure.

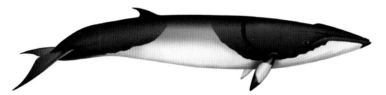

Bryde's Whale *Balaenoptera edeni* (winged-whale of Eden)

This baleen whale feeds all year round in tropical and subtropical waters. It is a high-speed, erratic swimmer and makes deep dives lasting over 8 minutes.

Diet: Small schooling fish, krill, plankton. **Surface behaviour:** Almost vertical breach with three-quarters of body visible, 4–7 blows before deep dive. Flukes rarely show when diving. May investigate boats. Strands occasionally. **Blow:** Single column 3–4 m.
Features: Dark grey back. Underside is purplish to creamy grey and may be mottled. Three longitudinal ridges on head. Baleen is black becoming white to light grey near snout. Curved dorsal fin beyond middle of back. Short, slender flippers, 40–70 white to yellowish throat grooves.
Length: 12–14 m. **Weight:** 12–20 t. **Status:** Secure.

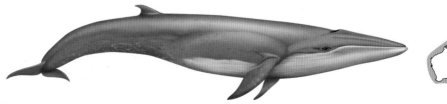

Blue Whale *Balaenoptera musculus* (muscular winged-whale)

This oceanic baleen whale is the largest of all living animals and was hunted to near extinction. They are commonly seen along the southern coast from November to May.

Diet: Krill, plankton. **Surface behaviour:** Adults seldom breach. Blows every 10–20 seconds for about 5 minutes before diving; flukes are exposed briefly at a low angle when diving. Strands occasionally.
Blow: Spectacular slender column up to 12 m.
Features: Varies from light blue with white mottling to uniform slate grey. Yellowish belly colour is caused by microscopic algae. Small, stubby dorsal fin located three-quarters of the way down the back. Broad, flat head with central ridge and 2 blowholes, 55–88 throat grooves. Black baleen. **Length:** 20–33 m. **Weight:** 100–120 t. **Status:** Endangered.

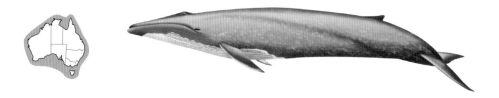

Sperm Whale *Physeter macrocephalus* (big-head blower)

The Sperm Whale is the largest toothed cetacean. It is known for its deep dives that can exceed 2000 m. Inside the huge head is a system of wax-filled tubes called spermaceti; this system controls buoyancy.

Diet: Cephalopods, fish. **Surface behaviour:** Breaches often, sometimes clearing the water. Spends 5–60 minutes on surface between dives. Breathes at 12–20 second intervals. Flukes and last third of body are exposed when diving. Lobtails. Occasional mass strandings.
Blow: Low, 2-m bushy blow angles forward. **Features:** Light to dark grey wrinkled skin; may have white blotched belly. Series of ridges on lower back. Large, square head with white lips. Short, stubby flippers, triangular tail flukes. Single blowhole on top left side of forehead. **Length:** 12–18 m. **Weight:** 20–50 t. **Status:** Secure.

Long-finned Pilot Whale *Globicephala melas* (black round-head)
Short-finned Pilot Whale *Globicephala macrorhynchus* (long-beaked round-head)

Pilot whales are very social mammals with matrilineal associations determining pod membership. The two species look much alike. The Long-finned frequents temperate waters, and the Short-finned is found in more tropical seas.

Diet: Cephalopods, fish. **Surface behaviour:** Seldom breaches. Takes several quick breaths before diving. Flukes may be exposed when diving. Logging, spyhopping, lobtailing, may bow-ride. Mass strandings. **Blow:** Strong squat blow to 1 m. **Features:** Black or dark grey above. Pale diagonal stripe behind each eye and grey or whitish cape on back. Greyish white patch on throat and belly. Bulbous head. Slender, sickle-shaped flippers. Curved dorsal fin with broad base forward of centre of back; shape varies with age and sex.
Length: SF 5.5–5.9 m, LF 5.5–6.5 m. **Weight:** SF 1–4 t, LF 1.8–3.5 t. **Status:** Secure.

☐ Short-finned
Pilot Whale
☐ Long-finned
Pilot Whale

Killer Whale *Orcinus orca* (whalelike whale)

These fast, efficient predators usually live in tight-knit family groups (pods) and each pod has its own dialect. They are often seen in coastal waters.

Diet: Fish, squid, seabirds, seals, other whales. **Surface behaviour:** Breaches often and clears surface. Spyhops, lobtails, slaps flippers and dorsal fin. Coordinated pod movement and logging. Mass strandings. **Blow:** Low squat blow.
Features: Compact, muscular body is jet black with a grey saddle patch behind dorsal fin. White patches behind eyes and on sides. Chin, belly and underside of tail flukes are white. Rounded paddle-shaped flippers. Male has a tall, almost straight dorsal fin up to 1.8 m long. Female fin is shorter and curved.
Length: 8–9.5 m. **Weight:** 2.6–9 t. **Status:** Secure.

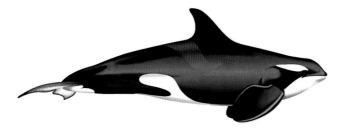

Common Dolphin *Delphinus delphis* (dolphin-like dolphin)

Common Dolphins are often seen in coastal waters. These fast, acrobatic cetaceans usually form large schools. Their high-pitched squeals can sometimes be heard from the surface.

Diet: Fish, marine invertebrates. **Surface behaviour:** Breaches, repetitive leaps, lobtails, slaps flippers and chin, bow-rides. Stranding is common. **Features:** Back is dark grey to black; belly is cream to white. Distinctive hourglass pattern on side is tan or yellowish near the head and grey near the tail. Black beak. Grey or black flippers and flukes. Relatively tall, curved dorsal fin at mid-back.
Length: 2.1–2.5 m.
Weight: 70–110 kg.
Status: Secure.

Bottlenose Dolphin *Tursiops truncatus* (shortened dolphin-face)

Bottlenose Dolphins usually live in small groups and there are complex social interactions within and amongst pods. They actively seek out boats and swimmers and can be seen in coastal waters all year round.

Diet: Fish, cephalopods and other marine invertebrates. **Surface behaviour:** Breaches and can clear water by several metres. Lobtails, bow-rides, body surfs. Will feed behind trawlers. May temporarily beach itself when chasing fish. Strands singly or in small groups.
Features: Blue-grey above grading to paler belly. Rounded forehead. Shork beak. Dark, slender, pointed flippers. Prominent curved dorsal fin in middle of back.
Length: 3–3.9 m. **Weight:** 150–650 kg. **Status:** Secure.

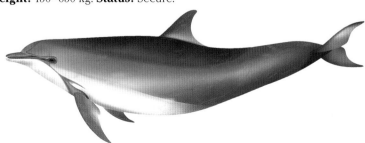

Australian Snubfin Dolphin *Orcaella heinsohni* (Heinsohn's little-whale)

This tropical dolphin favours shallow estuaries. It is distributed in northern Australia from the Brisbane River north to the Gulf of Carpentaria and west to at least Broome.

Diet: Fish, possibly squid and crustaceans. **Surface behaviour:** Slow moving, inconspicuous surfacing. Occasionally breaches and lobtails. Makes low horizontal leaps and occasionally spits out water when feeding. Three quick breaths between dives that last up to 1 minute. **Features:** Three colour pattern consisting of dark brown dorsal surface, lighter brown sides, white belly. Bulbous head and slight neck depression. Small, rounded dorsal fin three quarters down back. Large broad flippers. Broad flukes with distinct central notch. **Length:** 2.3–2.7 m. **Weight:** 90–130 kg. **Status:** Insufficiently known.

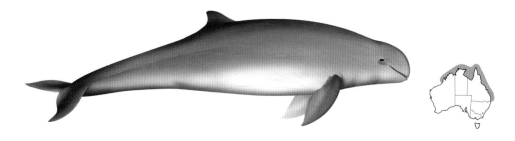

Indo-pacific Humpback Dolphin *Sousa chinensis* (Sousa of China)

This slow-swimming dolphin is often found close inshore and sometimes feeds behind trawlers. It is common in tropical waters, but ventures as far south as central NSW.

Diet: Fish, particularly schooling fish. **Surface behaviour:** Surfaces beak-first every 40 to 60 seconds. Breaches, lobtails, spyhops, flipper waves, back somersaults. Strands occasionally. **Features:** Pale to brownish grey or pinkish white above, grading to lighter underside. Long, slender beak and slightly rounded forehead. Low, triangular dorsal fin with base up to one-third of body length. Broad, round-tipped flippers.
Length: 2–2.8 m. **Weight:** 150–200 kg. **Status:** Secure.

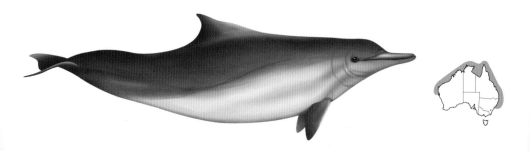

Striped Dolphin *Stenella coeruleoalba* (sky-blue white stenella)

This very active dolphin travels in large pods. Its shallow dives last 5 to 10 seconds, but it is capable of longer dives up to 200 m when feeding.

Diet: Fish, squid. **Surface behaviour:** Breaches. Leaps up to 7 m above the surface. Somersaults, tail-spins. Seldom bow-rides. Strands occasionally.
Features: Upper back ranges from dark bluish grey to brownish grey becoming paler grey near tail. Curved dorsal fin in middle of back. Sides are grey and belly is pinkish white. Prominent dark beak. Dark side stripe from eye to anus. Dark stripe from eye to flipper. Slender dark flippers.
Length: 2.5–3.2 m. **Weight:** 90–150 kg. **Status:** Secure.

Long-snouted Spinner Dolphin *Stenella longirostris* (long-beaked stenella)

This oceanic dolphin congregates in large schools and is well known for its aerial displays. There have been no recorded strandings in Australia.

Diet: Fish, cephalopods. **Surface behaviour:** Clears surface by up to 3 m when breaching. Vertical twists and horizontal spins when leaping. Bow-rides.
Features: Dark grey above with pale grey sides. Lower jaw, throat and belly are white. Dark stripe from eye to base of flipper. Long slender flippers are dark. Long slim beak. Tall triangular dorsal fin.
Length: 1.8–2 m. **Weight:** 45–75 kg. **Status:** Secure.

Introduced Mammals

Ever since Europeans began mapping, exploiting and recolonising Australia they have been bringing their homeland animals with them. Most were considered necessary to human survival in an isolated and alien land. Others, such as the notorious House Mouse, Sewer Rat and Black Rat arrived as stowaways. Those that jumped ship, escaped or were released prospered in the absence of their natural predators.

This sudden and recent invasion of placental mammals, including humans, has had a dramatic effect on Australia's fragile ecosystems. Native mammals find their long-term survival prospects diminishing as their habitats and ecological niches are usurped by introduced placental mammals.

✗ A female cat producing four female kittens a year could have 2 million female descendants in 10 years if each generation reproduced at the same rate.

✗ Over 1,400 Feral Cats were removed from Peron Peninsula in Shark Bay, Western Australia during a 3-year cull.

✗ Camels eat more than 230 species of native plants.

✗ The Red Fox is a voracious predator of small marsupials.

✗ There are over 1.5 million feral Donkeys in Australia.

✗ The Feral Pig is also known as the Razorback or Captain Cooker.

✗ A female Feral Goat can breed at the age of six months.

Feral animals, such as the goat (opposite) and cat (top right) compete with native animals and destroy fragile ecosystems. The foxes above have been shot in an attempt to eradicate them.

Feral Dog *Canis lupus familiaris*

Various breeds of domestic dog have been introduced to Australia as companions and working animals. Those that have escaped their domestic ties and live in the wild are referred to as feral. They are capable of breeding twice a year and of interbreeding with the Dingo. These predators hunt in packs and do not always eat what they kill.

Wildlife threat: Preys on native animals and competes with them for food and shelter. Carries diseases that can infect native species. Interbreeding may lead to extinction of the Dingo.

Red Fox *Vulpes vulpes*

The Red Fox was released near Melbourne in 1845 for sport hunting. It is now one of the most widespread introduced mammals, occurring in most habitats except in the northern tropics. It is an opportunistic carnivore that feeds on mammals, birds, reptiles and insects, and it does not always eat what it kills. Foxes breed in early winter and produce litters of 4 or more young that are independent by late summer.

Wildlife threats: Preys on native fauna and competes with native mammals for food and shelter.

Feral Cat *Felis catus*

Cats were first introduced to Australia by sea traders and explorers. European settlers boosted cat numbers by the thousands, not only as domestic pets but as a solution to introduced rodents and Rabbit plagues. Feral Cats can be found in all habitats and it is estimated there are more than 12 million. A cat eats anything up to its own size and scavenges when live prey is scarce. A female can produce three litters a year with an average of 5 per litter.

Wildlife threats: Competes for food and shelter. Preys on native animals. Carries diseases such as toxoplasmosis that can infect native carnivores.

Rabbit *Oryctolagus cuniculus*

In 1859 a landowner at Winchelsea, Victoria, released 24 Rabbits for sport hunting. They have since spread to all regions except the tropical north. Rabbits live in separate male and female groups during the breeding season. They produce 1 to 5 litters per year with 4 to 5 babies per litter. They feed on the leaves and roots of grass, ground covers and shrubs.

Wildlife threats: Competes for food and shelter. Feeding habits destroy native vegetation that supports wildlife.

Black Rat *Rattus rattus*

The Black Rat is found in urban, agricultural and natural habitats around the coast of Australia. They have a lifespan of about 1 year, during which time a female can produce up to six litters of 5–10 young. These omnivorous rodents are capable climbers and swimmers. They are carriers of diseases that can be transmitted to humans.

Wildlife threats: Competes for food and shelter. Preys on small native animals.

Fallow Deer *Dama dama*

This is one of six species of deer that have become established in Australia. The Fallow Deer was introduced by the landed gentry for sport hunting. These grazing herbivores prefer open forest, woodland and grassland habitats. They live in groups and are usually active during the day. A single young is born every year, or, very rarely, twins.

Wildlife threats: Competes with native herbivores for food and shelter. Alters wildlife habitats by selective grazing and soil compaction.

Donkey *Equus asinus*

The donkey was introduced in 1866 for use as a pack animal, especially in the arid regions of South Australia and Western Australia. They were released to fend for themselves when motorised transport became more reliable. During the dry season they congregate near fresh water, forming herds of up to 500.

Wildlife threat: Competes for food. Close cropping and soil compaction destroys shelter for small ground and burrowing animals. Vegetation destruction also leads to soil erosion.

Brumby *Equus caballus*

These escapees from the rural workforce are derived from various stock including Arabian, thoroughbred and draught horses. Most are found in arid and semi-arid grasslands with permanent water supplies. Brumbies in the alpine high plains are smaller, heavier and more agile.

Wildlife threat: Competes for food. Close cropping, over grazing and soil compaction destroys wildlife habitats and causes soil erosion. Also fouls water sources.

One-humped Camel *Camelus dromedarius*

The One-humped Camel or Dromedary lives in herds of up to several hundred in the sandy deserts of central and western Australia. About 10,000 were introduced between 1840 and 1907 as beasts of burden. Their descendants were released when no longer needed. These aridland specialists eat succulents and other ground plants and browse on saltbush and acacia shrubs. They can store six months worth of food energy in their humps, which can account for 200 kg of body weight. A thirsty camel can suck up 100 L of water in one go.

Wildlife threat: Eats plants that feed and shelter native animals.

Feral Pig *Sus scrofa*

This is another First Fleeter that has spread throughout much of northern and eastern Australia. It is usually black with a coarse mane that stands erect when it is alarmed. They are voracious omnivores that hunt small mammals and rip up the soil in search of plant food.

Wildlife threats: Eats native fauna. Competes for food. Its wallowing fouls water sources. Changes wildlife habitats by destroying native vegetation and soil surface.

Feral Goat *Capra hircus*

Goats arrived with the First Fleet in 1788 to be used as a source of meat and milk. They are now well established in semi-arid habitats where rocky hills and dense scrub offer shelter and where fresh water is available.

Wildlife threat: Competes for food, shelter and water. Selective feeding habits and over grazing change wildlife habitats and cause soil erosion.

Swamp Buffalo *Bubalus bubalis*

The Swamp Buffalo was first brought to Australia from Indonesia in 1826 as a source of meat for settlers at Fort Dundas on Melville Island. More imports were then released on the mainland. It lives in permanent and seasonal wetlands across the top end of the Northern Territory. These sedentary grazers feed on terrestrial and water plants and form herds of up to 500.

Wildlife threats: Competes for food and shelter. Feeding and semi-aquatic behaviour destroy wetland habitats.

Daintree River
Ringtail Possum
Pseudochirulus cinereus

✗ Use binoculars.

✗ Listen as well
as look.

✗ Wear clothes that
don't flap or rustle.

✗ Move slowly,
smoothly and
quietly.

✗ Track against
the wind.

✗ Freeze when an
animal sees you;
move when
it relaxes.

✗ Leave the family dog
at home.

✗ Do not try to
catch or handle
Australian native
mammals, even
those accustomed
to the presence of
humans. They will
defend themselves
if threatened or
frightened. Teeth,
claws, kicks and
lashing tails can
inflict injuries. Treat
them with caution
and respect.

MAMMALS AND PEOPLE
Watching Wildlife

Many Australian mammals are small and are active only at night, so it is not always easy finding them in their own homes. The more you know about an animal's appearance, habits and haunts, the greater the chance of seeing one in the wild.

Start by visiting zoos, wildlife sanctuaries and aquariums to get a better idea of the sizes, shapes and colours of Australian mammals. The exhibits, demonstrations and interpretive signs offer a wealth of information about animal behaviour.

In the wild, it is a case of being in the right place at the right time. Dusk and dawn are the best times on land because this is when many mammals move to and from their feeding places. Creeks, waterholes and the edges of habitats are usually the action hot spots. Animals have keen senses, but if you keep still and blend in with the landscape they may ignore you.

Guided tours in national parks and visits to wildlife sanctuaries provide introductions to many native mammals.

Identifying Mammals

It is usually easy to identify a mammal, such as a wallaby, as a member of a group, but it can be difficult to tell just which species it is. Take a notebook when you go wildlife watching, and make notes and drawings of your sightings. Look for tracks and scats. The more information you record, the easier it will be to find the animal and its scientific name. You can eliminate some species by their habitat and distribution.

Things to Note

Size – compare size to an animal you know.
Shape – describe shape of head, body, limbs, tail, etc.
Colour – note the colours and patterns on body parts.
Behaviour – what is the animal doing?
Calls – what noises is it making?
Habitat – describe the place where you see the animal.

Tracks, Scats and Other Signs

When out walking look for:
footprints;
scats (animal droppings);
scratches on the ground and tree trunks;
holes in the ground;
fur caught on branches or smooth rubbing posts;
well-worn pathways.

Wild animals can become accustomed to people, especially when food is offered.

Some Zoos, Fauna Parks & Sanctuaries

Search the internet for zoos, fauna parks, wildlife sanctuaries.

Australian Capital Territory
National Zoo & Aquarium
Tidbinbilla Nature Reserve

New South Wales
Featherdale Wildlife Park
Scotia Earth Sanctuary
Sydney Aquarium
Taronga Zoo
Western Plains Zoo
Yellow Pinch Wildlife Park

Victoria
Healesville Sanctuary
Little River Earth Sanctuary
Melbourne Zoo
Melbourne Wildlife Sanctuary
Pearcedale Conservation Park
Phillip Island Nature Park
Werribee Open Range Zoo

Tasmania
Bonorong Wildlife Park
Trowunna Wildlife Park

South Australia
Adelaide Zoo
Cleland Wildlife Park
Monarto Zoo
Warrawong Earth Sanctuary

Western Australia
Caversham Wildlife Park
Marapana Wildlife Park
Perth Zoo
Wave Rock Wildlife Park

Northern Territory
Alice Springs Desert Park
Territory Wildlife Park

Queensland
Australia Zoo
Cairns Tropical Zoo
Currumbin Wildlife Sanctuary
Daisy Hill Koala Centre
David Fleay Wildlife Park
Lone Pine Koala Sanctuary
Rainforest Habitat Wildlife
  Sanctuary

✘ Your subjects will not stand still and pose for the camera. Have patience.

✘ While auto focus does work at night, manual focus gives better control. Move back or forward to make minor focus adjustments.

✘ To select the best angle for colour, form and texture, try moving around your subject to view it from different angles.

✘ Pay some attention to backgrounds. Images may be greatly enhanced by aesthetically pleasing backgrounds.

✘ Harsh sunlight creates dark shadows, but on a bright overcast day, light is softened so that detail of fur and markings are defined.

✘ If the light level is very low, requiring a slow shutter speed (below $^1/_{30}$ sec.), a tripod may be needed to hold the camera steady.

✘ For best results with an inexpensive point-and-snap camera, you need to be within 1–3 m of your subject.

Photographing Wildlife

Photographing mammals is a great challenge for novice and experienced nature photographers. The more you know about an animal and its behaviour, the more likely you are to find it in the wild.

Understanding behaviour will help you to interpret what is happening and possibly predict the animal's next move. Some nocturnal or shy species may be elusive, but you can photograph their tracks, their homes and other evidence of their presence.

Knowledge of your subject will also be useful when you choose your equipment. You need to consider, for instance, lighting for photographing nocturnal animals and lenses for size and distance.

Knowledge of your subjects will add depth and meaning to your photography. For example, an image of a wallaby can be a portrait; it can also be a study of behaviour.

A study of a female and juvenile Whiptail Wallaby.

Equipment

For mammal photography, 35 mm SLR cameras are best. For daylight work on macropods and marine mammals, use lenses between 400 mm and 600 mm, and for night work a 80–200 mm zoom with a power flash, or sometimes two, depending on the conditions and the subject.

Other useful equipment includes: a tripod when using long lenses and slow shutter speeds; and a head torch and a focus lantern for photographing nocturnal mammals.

A photographer wearing a head torch.

In Captivity

The most important rule for photographing animals in fauna parks and zoos when the day is bright and sunny is "don't bother". The light on a bright overcast day is best for image clarity and detail. Such conditions may bring cooler weather making wildlife more active, and nocturnal animals may even put in an appearance.

At some fauna parks and zoos, you can mingle with large macropods in open enclosures. These animals are used to people and you can get good close-up shots.

Although the animals are captive, they are most active early in the morning and late in the afternoon, so plan to be there at the times of year when the days are shortest. If the gates open at 9 a.m. and close at 5 p.m., aim to start at 3 p.m. for best results. Using a telephoto lens (preferably 300–500 mm), you will be able to obtain the best portrait or behavioural shots.

✘ In a film camera, a motor drive helps capture magic moments when animals assume interesting postures.

✘ Use the high resolution setting on digital cameras.

✘ Use a telephoto lens, as long a focal-length as possible, to soften backgrounds and, in some cases, the immediate foreground if you are shooting through a wire cage.

✘ Be prepared to wait for as long as it takes for the animal to assume an interesting posture.

✘ A flash for fill may be useful; shoot on cool, bright overcast days.

Captive animals interacting with their carers can make interesting images.

✘ It can take some time for animals to become accustomed to your presence in a hide. They are likely to catch your scent, and it can take days for them to show up.

✘ If you are fortunate enough to live in an area where mammals might visit your home, you can treat your house as a hide for photography, and provide shelters, such as nesting boxes.

In the Wild

Photographing native mammals in the wild requires patience and preparation. Learn all you can about your subjects to have the best chance of getting the images you desire. For instance, large macropods may be well camouflaged, but they are big enough to be seen by a keen-eyed photographer who knows what to look for and where. Be as unobtrusive as possible and move slowly: sudden movement will startle wild creatures.

A telephoto lens is invaluable in this situation because it magnifies distant objects and you can photograph animals without disturbing them. It is also handy for capturing tree-dwellers as a long lens will bring the animal's image to you.

Depicting motion is an exciting challenge. A high shutter speed (say, $^1/_{1000}$ sec.) will give a pin-sharp subject that appears frozen in time. A slow shutter speed ($^1/_5$–$^1/_{30}$ sec.) will record movement as a blur. Panning the camera can be effective because both subject and background will be blurred, as in the photograph of the Eastern Grey Kangaroo below. For sharp surrounds and blurred action, put the camera on a tripod and set the shutter at about $^1/_{10}$ sec.

Top left and right, bottom left: Photographing wildlife on foot, from a car, from a hide.
Bottom right: The quarry.

At Night

You will need to be familiar with the habits of the more elusive nocturnal species to know when and where to find them. You also need a good torch to track down animals by their reflected eyeshine and to provide light for focusing the camera.

While reflected eyeshine is useful for locating animals and even identifying different species, it is not a good photographic effect. See the photography tips at right for ways to avoid it.

Be prepared to fire off a few quick shots before your subject takes off.

Plan ahead, assemble all the necessary equipment, clothes and packs, and give yourself plenty of time. Stumbling around in the dark and fumbling for equipment is the surest way to cause nocturnal mammals to melt into the night.

A diver entices a curious fur-seal.

Under Water

Photographing a marine mammal in its underwater habitat is another exciting challenge for avid wildlife photographers. Natural light is limited and wary animals will keep their distance. However seals, dolphins and Dugongs are inquisitive and often investigate divers at close range.

A wide-angle 15 mm or 20 mm lens and a flash for fill-in lighting are recommended whether using an amphibious camera or a camera in underwater housing.

✘ Take the time to master the use of electronic flash for best night-time results. Practise on spiders, frogs and possums, or any other wild creatures you find in your own backyard.

✘ A head-mounted torch, such as miners or anglers wear, is useful to locate animals after dark. Their eyes reflect the torch light. Some knowledge of colour of eyeshine can be useful in identifying subjects.

✘ Some compact cameras eliminate red-eye reflections automatically.

✘ You can avoid reflected eyeshine by holding a detachable flash away from the lens's angle of view.

✘ The red-eye problem can be corrected when editing digital images on computer.

✘ Photographing under water at night also calls for an electronic flash to provide the light source and an underwater lantern to find the quarry and give enough light for focus.

Colony of Black Flying-fox
Pteropus alecto

Water-rat
Hydromys chrysogaster

Bottlenose Dolphin
Tursiops truncatus

Southern Brown Bandicoot
Isoodon obesulus

Lumholtz's Tree-kangaroo
Dendrolagus lumholtzi

Short-eared Brushtail Possum
Trichosurus caninus

Koala and young
Phascolarctos cinereus

Brush-tailed Phascogale
Phascogale tapoatafa

Platypus
Ornithorhynchus anatinus

Western Grey Kangaroo
Macropus fuliginosus

Short-beaked Echidna
Tachyglossus aculeatus

Common Wombat
Vombatus ursinus

Australia Sea-lion and pup
Neophoca cinerea

Northern Hairy-nosed
Wombat

Survival Threats

While any of the
following factors can
threaten the survival of
a species, it is usually a
combination of factors
that leads to extinction:

• habitat destruction or
change;

• introduced animals;

• disease;

• exploitation;

• natural disasters;

• climate change.

Long-nosed Potoroo

Wildlife Conservation

Australia holds the world record for mammal extinctions. In just
over 200 years 27 species of Australian mammals have become
extinct. Ten of those extinctions have occurred in the last 25
years.

Extinction is a natural process in an ever-changing world
where living organisms use and recycle the Earth's finite
resources. Apart from cataclysmic events, it is also a gradual
process. However, the current rate of extinction has increased
considerably because of human activities. When humans
change the land to suit their own purposes, they also change
its finely balanced ecosystems. Loss of habitat combined with
predation and competition from introduced animals are the
most serious threats to the survival of Australia's remaining
mammals. Looking after Australia, its oceans and wildlife helps
maintain the world's biological diversity, making the Earth a
healthy place for all living things.

Status Terms

Extinct in the Wild
A species is presumed extinct in the wild if there has
been no confirmed sighting in the past 50 years.

Critically Endangered
A species faces a high risk of extinction in the immediate
future.

Endangered
A species faces a high risk of extinction in the near
future.

Vulnerable
A species faces a high risk of extinction in the medium-
term future.

Secure
Current numbers and distribution indicate no risk of
extinction in the present environmental conditions.

The listing of a mammal as a threatened species and its
conservation status can vary between Federal, State and
Territory Governments.

National parks and other conservation reserves provide habitats for native animals.

Scientific research provides information about native animals and their survival requirements.

Education promotes awareness of native animals and understanding of their importance.

Captive breeding and reintroduction programs offer threatened species a second chance.

Reducing the Risk

Anyone can lend a hand in helping native mammals survive. Reducing the risk of extinction can be as simple as:

- learning about locally occurring native mammals and their habitat requirements;
- planting native trees and shrubs in the garden;
- confining domestic pets at night;
- not dumping unwanted pets in the wild;
- avoiding the use of chemical pesticides and herbicides;
- joining a community group to clean up and revegetate bushland.

Planting at Paringa, SA.

Cobourg Marine Park
Gurig
Cape Hotham
Wildman Reserve
Manton Dam
Litchfield
Kakadu
Ashmore Reef
Nitmiluk
Elsey
Bar
Drysdale River
Ord River
Prince Regent
Keep River
Gregory
Point Coulomb
Purnululu
Connells Lagoon
Camooweal Ca
Dragon Tree Soak
Barrow Island
Millstream-Chichester
Mungaroona Range
Rudall River
Arltunga
Ruby Gap
West MacDonnell
Finke Gorge
Karijini
Cape Range
Watarrka
Ningaloo
Barlee Range
Uluru-Kata Tjuta
Mount Augustus
Collier Range
Gibson Desert
Kennedy Range
Simps
Des
Bernier & Dorre
Island
Shark Bay
Witjira
Francois Peron
De La Poer
Neale Junction
Tallaringa
La
Zuytdorp
Wanjarri
Yeo Lake
Elliot Price
Toolonga
Kalbarri
Wandana
Great Victoria Desert
Plumridge Lakes
S
Gammon
Mount Manning Range
Goongarrie
Nullarbor
Lake Torrens
Alexander Morrison
Karroun Hill
Queen Victoria Spring
Beekeepers
Walyahmoning
Lesueur
Watheroo
Nullarbor
Lake Gairdner
Lake
Badgingarra
Boorabbin
Pinkawillinie
Nambung
Moore River
Jilbadji
Dundas
Bascombe Well
Julimar
Frank Hann
Nuytsland
Dragon Rocks
Monadnocks
Coffin Bay
Hincks
Chinocup
Peak Charles
Lane Poole
Lincoln
Yalgorup
Dunn Rock
Cape Arid
Innes
Leeuwin Naturaliste
Lake Magenta
Stokes
Cape Le Grand
Flinders Chase
Shannon
Fitzgerald River
Cape Gantheaume
D'Entrecasteaux
Stirling Range
Coc
Mount Frankland
C
Walpole-Nornalup
Lower

National Park

Marine Park

Other reserve

0   200   400   600 km

Top National Parks

NSW
Kosciuszko NP
Warrumbungle NP
Jervis Bay NP

ACT
Namadgi NP

Vic
Grampians NP
Otway NP
Wilson's Promontory NP

Tas
Cradle Mt-Lake St Clair NP
Freycinet NP
Mt Field NP

SA
Flinders Chase NP
Flinders Ranges NP
Nullarbor NP

WA
Cape Range NP
Leeuwin-Naturaliste NP

NT
Kakadu NP
West Macdonnell NP

Qld
Daintree NP
Lamington NP
Simpson Desert NP

References and Further Information

Books

Beattie, Andrew J.(ed). 1995. *Australia's Biodiversity: Living Wealth.* Reed Books, Sydney.

Breckwoldt, R. 1988. *The Dingo: A Very Elegant Animal.* Angus & Robertson, Sydney.

Bryden M., *et al.* 1998. *Dugongs, Whales, Dolphins and Seals: A Guide to the Sea Mammals of Australia.* Allen & Unwin, Sydney.

Carwardine, Mark. 1996. *Whales Dolphins and Porpoises.* Dorling Kindersley, London.

Churchill, Sue. 1998. *Australian Bats.* Reed New Holland, Sydney.

Cronin, L. 1987. *Koala: Australia's Endearing Marsupial.* Leonard Cronin/Reed Books, Sydney.

Healy, Janet (ed.). 1997. *Encyclopedia of Australian Wildlife.* Reader's Digest, Sydney.

Jones, Cath (comp.). 2003. *Handbook of Australian Wildlife.* Steve Parish Publishing, Brisbane.

Lindenmayer, David. 2002. *Gliders of Australia: A Natural History.* UNSW Press, Sydney.

Long, J., *et al.* 2002. *Prehistoric Mammals of Australia and New Guinea.* University of New South Wales Press, Sydney.

Menkhorst, P., Knight, F. 2001. *Field Guide to the Mammals of Australia.* Oxford University Press, Melbourne.

Slater, Pat. 1997. *Amazing Facts about Australian Mammals.* Steve Parish Publishing, Brisbane.

Slater, Pat. 2000. *Encyclopedia of Australian Animals.* Steve Parish Publishing, Brisbane.

Strahan, Ronald (ed.). 1992. *Encyclopedia of Australian Animals: Mammals.* Angus & Robertson/Australian Museum, Sydney

Strahan, Ronald (Ed). 2002. *The Mammals of Australia.* Reed New Holland, Sydney.

Triggs, Barbara. 2004. *Tracks, Scats and Other Traces: A Field Guide to Australian Mammals.* Rev. Edn. Oxford University Press, Melbourne.

Tucker, Mark. 1989. *Whales and Whale Watching in Australia.* ANPWS, Canberra.

Van Oosterzee, Penny (ed). 1998. *A Field Guide to Central Australia.* JB Books, SA.

Websites

There are many informative Australian mammals websites. Some are listed below.

Museums

National guide to collecting institutions: amol.org.au/guide/index.asp

Federal: www.nma.gov.au

Adelaide: www.samuseum.sa.gov.au

Brisbane: www.qmuseum.qld.gov.au

Canberra: www.arts.act.gov.au/

Darwin: www.dcdsca.nt.gov.au

Hobart: www.tmag.tas.gov.au

Melbourne: www.melbourne.museum.vic.gov.au

Perth: www.museum.wa.gov.au

Sydney: www.austmus.gov.au

Townsville: www.mtq.qld.gov.au

Government Environment Agencies

Federal: www.deh.gov.au

ACT: www.environment.act.gov.au

NSW: www.epa.nsw.gov.au; www.nationalparks.nsw.gov.au

NT: www.nt.gov.au/ntg/environ.shtml

Qld: www.epa.qld.gov.au

SA: www.dehaa.sa.gov.au

Tas: www.parks.tas.gov.au; www.dpiwe.tas.gov.au

Vic: www.parkweb.vic.gov.au

WA: www.calm.wa.gov.au

Other sites

Australian Conservation Foundation: www.acfonline.org.au

Australian Mammal Society: www.australianmammals.org.au

Australian Marine Conservation Society: www.amcs.org.au

www.australianwildlife.com.au

www.csiro.au

Marsupial Society of Australia: www.marsupialsociety.org

www.westernwildlife.com.au

Wilderness Society: www.wilderness.org.au

Whales of Australia: www.upstarts.net.au/site/non_commercial/whales.html

Glossary

amphibious Living on land and in water.

aquatic Living in fresh or salt water.

arboreal Living in trees.

arid land Land that gets less than 250 mm rain per year; desert.

brigalow *Acacia harpophylla;* open forest dominated by brigalow or similar, 10–15 m high.

carnivore An animal that eats animals.

cloaca Posterior chamber of the gut where the urinary tract and female reproductive system also end in monotremes and marsupials.

closed forest Forest having canopy coverage greater than 80% of land area.

crepuscular Active at dawn and dusk.

desert Land that gets less than 350 mm rain per year.

diapause, embryonic State of arrested development in a viable embryo which may be carried in the uterus for some months.

digit Finger or toe.

distribution Area within which a species occurs.

diurnal Active during the day.

echolocation Sensing objects by sending out sounds then analysing the echoes reflected after they impact.

embryo Animal in developmental stage between conception and birth.

feral Having reverted to a wild state.

forest Area having high-density tree cover.

gestation Time between conception and birth.

gibber plain Flat, arid terrain covered with smooth, rounded stones

gregarious Living in a group.

heathland Vegetation dominated by small shrubs growing on poor, sandy soils.

herbivore Animal that eats plants.

home range Area an animal traverses during its normal daily activities.

larynx Part of windpipe containing vocal chords.

mallee Small multi-stemmed eucalypts that often dominate semi-arid and arid areas.

matrilineal Inherited from the mother or traced through the female line.

monsoon forest Tropical forest of trees, vines and shrubs watered by monsoon rains; may contain some deciduous species.

mulga woodland Area, usually arid or semi-arid, dominated by *Acacia aneura*, a small tree, or similar species.

nocturnal Active at night.

omnivore Animal that eats plants and animals.

open forest Forest having canopy coverage less than 80% of land area.

patagium In a gliding mammal, the membrane between fore- and hindlimbs that stretches to allow volplaning.

pelt Skin and fur of an animal.

predator Animal that hunts and eats animals.

prehensile Able to grip.

rainforest Forest of tall trees with crowns almost touching to form a closed canopy.

recurved Bent backwards.

savanna Land across tropical northern Australia covered with dense grass and scattered trees.

scavenger Animal that eats dead animals.

scrubland Land covered with dense vegetation predominantly consisting of stunted trees, low-growing shrubs and non-woody plants.

semi-arid land Land that gets 250–350 mm rain per year.

shrubland Land dominated by woody vegetation, generally more than 0.5 m and less than 5 m in height, approximately.

terrestrial Living on land.

territorial Related to the defence of a territory.

territory Area occupied and defended by an individual or group.

volplane To glide through the air.

wetland Land that is regularly wet or flooded, being covered with fresh, brackish or salt water for part of each year.

woodland Area sparsely covered with trees.

Index of Common Names

Antechinus, Brown 40
  Fawn 40, 44
  Yellow-footed 11, 30, 45
Bandicoot 54–57
  Barred, Eastern 60
  Barred, Western 55, 59
  Brown, Northern 54, 58
  Brown, Southern 59, 204
  Golden 58
  Long-nosed 55, 60
  Spiny, Rufous 61
Bat, Ghost 150, 151, 155
  Tube-nosed, Eastern 154
  Wattled, Hoary 157
Bettong, Brush-tailed 108,
  114, 117
  Burrowing 114, 116
  Rufous 114, 116
Biggada, *see* Wallaroo,
  Common
Bilby 54–57, 61
  Lesser 56
Blossom-bat, Common 148,
  154
Brumby 196
Buffalo, Water 197
Camel, One-humped 196
Cat, Feral 192, 194
Chuditch 31
Cuscus, Common,
    Southern 97
  Common Spotted
  98
Dalgyte 56
Deer, Fallow 195
Devil, Tasmanian 30, 36–39
Dibbler, Southern 43
Dingo 13, 30, 147, 166–169
Dog, Feral 194

Dolphin, Bottlenose 178,
    180, 182, 189, 204
  Common 189
  Humpback, Indo-
    Pacific 190
  Australian Snubfin 179,
    190
  Spinner, Long-snouted 191
  Striped 191
Donkey 196
Dugong 176–177
Dunnart, Fat-tailed 40, 47
  Hairy-footed 41
  Red-cheeked 47
Echidna, Short-beaked 11,
  19, 24–27, 205
Euro, *see* Wallaroo,
  Common
Field-rat, Pale 165
Flying-fox, Black 149, 152,
  204
  Grey-headed 13, 153
  Red, Little 153
  Spectacled 148, 152
Fox, Red 192, 194
Fur-seal, Australian 170, 171,
  173, 175
  New Zealand 12, 170, 171,
  175
Glider, Feathertail 79, 102
  Greater 79, 81, 90, 92
  Mahogany 86, 89
  Squirrel 63, 78, 79, 80, 86,
  89
  Sugar 76, 80, 86, 88
  Yellow-bellied 86, 88
Goat, Feral 192, 197
Hare-wallaby, Banded 118
  Central 118

  Eastern 118
  Rufous 118, 119
  Spectacled 119
Hopping-mouse, Spinifex
  158, 162
Horse, feral see Brumby
Itjaritjari 52
Kangaroo, Grey, Eastern 29,
  106, 110, 112, 136, 144
  Grey, Western 136, 144,
  205
  Hill, *see* Wallaroo,
  Common
  Red 106, 110, 112, 137, 145
Koala 7, 12, 29, 64–69, 204
Kowari 30, 40, 42
Kultarr 46
Leafnosed-bat, Diadem 155
  Orange 156
Melomys, Grassland 161
Mole, Marsupial,
    Southern 52–53
Monjon 130
Mouse, Ash-grey 162
  Delicate 164
  Long-tailed 158
  New Holland 158
  Pebble-mound, Kakadu
  163
Mulgara 41, 42
Myotis, Large-footed 157
Nabarlek 128, 130
Ninu 56
Numbat 30, 48–51
Pademelon, Red-legged 12,
  121
  Red-necked 120, 121
  Tasmanian 120

Phascogale, Brush-tailed 40, 45, 205
Pig, Feral 192, 197
Planigale, Common 46
  Long-tailed 40
Platypus 19, 20–23, 205
Possums 76–103
  Brushtail, Common 76. 80, 96, 99
  Brushtail, Mountain 76, 96
  Brushtail, Short-eared 78, 96, 98, 204
  Honey 100
  Leadbeater's 80, 86, 87
  Ringtail, Common 7, 76, 90, 95
  Ringtail, Daintree River 94, 198
  Ringtail, Green 76, 80, 90, 93
  Ringtail, Herbert River 79, 90, 94,
  Ringtail, Lemuroid 90, 92
  Ringtail, Rock 76, 90, 93
  Ringtail, Western 90, 95
  Scaly-tailed 96, 99
  Striped 81, 86, 87
Potoroo, Long-footed 114, 115
  Long-nosed 108, 114, 115
Pseudantechinus, Fat-tailed 44
  Sandstone 40, 43
Pygmy-possum, Eastern 82, 85
  Little 82, 85
  Long-tailed 78, 83
  Mountain 81, 82, 84
  Western 84

Quokka 122
Quoll 30–35
  Eastern 11, 31, 32, 33, 35
  Northern 31, 32, 33, 34
  Spotted-tailed 31, 32, 33, 35
  Western 31, 33, 34
Rabbit 195
Rat, Black 195
  Bush 164
  Dusky 158
  Plains 163
  Stick-nest, Greater 13, 161
  White-tailed, Giant 158
Rat-kangaroo, Musky 114, 117
Rock-rat, Common 165
Rock-wallabies 126–128
  Allied 129
  Black-footed 126, 128, 131
  Brush-tailed 128, 132
  Mareeba 128, 131
  Proserpine 133
  Purple-necked 126
  Short-eared 129
  Yellow-footed 133
Seal, Elephant, Southern 174
Sea-lion, Australian 5, 147, 170, 171, 173, 174, 205
Sheathtail-bat, Common 156
Thylacine 30,
Tiger, Tasmanian 30,
Tree-kangaroo, Bennett's 125
  Lumholtz's 124, 125, 204
Tree-rat, Brush-tailed 160
Wallaby, Agile 112, 138
  Black-striped 138
  Brush, Western 139

Nailtail, Bridled 134, 135
Nailtail, Northern 135
Parma 140
Red-necked 108, 141
Swamp 123
Tammar 139
Toolache 136
Whiptail 112, 137, 140, 200
Wallaroo, Antilopine 113, 142
  Black 105, 113, 142
  Common 10, 113, 137, 143
  Grey, Eastern, see Wallaroo, Common
  Red, see Wallaroo, Common
Walpatjirri 56
Water-rat 158, 160, 204
Whale, Blue 178, 181, 182, 187
  Bryde's 186
  Dwarf Minke 186
  Humpback 179, 181, 182, 185
  Killer 178, 180, 182, 188
  Pilot, Long-finned 188
  Pilot, Short-finned 188
  Right, Southern 178, 179, 181, 182, 185
  Sperm 178, 179, 180, 182, 187
Wombat 70–75
  Common 70, 71, 74, 205
  Hairy-nosed, Northern 75, 206
  Hairy-nosed, Southern 63, 70, 73, 75
Woylie 114

Index of Scientific Names

Acrobates pygmaeus 102
Aepyprymnus rufescens 114, 116
Antechinomys laniger 46
Antechinus bellus 44
Antechinus flavipes 30, 45
Arctocephalus forsteri 175
Arctocephalus pusillus 175
Balaenoptera acutorostrata 186
Balaenoptera edeni 186
Balaenoptera musculus 187
Bettongia lesueur 116
Bettongia penicillata 117
Bubalus bubalis 197
Burramys parvus 83
Camelus dromedarius 196
Canis lupus familiaris 194
Canis lupus dingo 169
Capra hircus 197
Cercartetus caudatus 84
Cercartetus concinnus 84
Cercartetus lepidus 85
Cercartetus nanus 82, 85
Chalinolobus nigrogriseus 157
Conilurus penicillatus 160
Dactylopsila trivirgata 87
Dama dama 195
Dasycercus cristicauda 42
Dasyuroides byrnei 42
Dasyurus geoffroii 34
Dasyurus hallucatus 34
Dasyurus maculatus 35
Dasyurus viverrinus 35
Delphinus delphis 189

Dendrolagus bennettianus 125
Dendrolagus lumholtzi 124, 125, 204
Dugong dugon 177
Echymipera rufescens 61
Equus asinus 196
Equus caballus 196
Eubalaena australis 185
Felis catus 194
Globicephala macrorhynchus 188
Globicephala melas 188
Gymnobelideus leadbeateri 80, 87
Hemibelideus lemuroides 92
Hipposideros diadema 155
Hydromys chrysogaster 160, 204
Hypsiprymnodon moschatus 117
Isoodon auratus 58
Isoodon macrourus 58
Isoodon obesulus 59, 204
Lagorchestes conspicillatus 119
Lagorchestes hirsutus 118, 119
Lasiorhinus krefftii 75
Lasiorhinus latifrons 75
Leporillus conditor 161
Macroderma gigas 150, 155
Macropus agilis 138
Macropus antilopinus 142
Macropus bernardus 142
Macropus dorsalis 138

Macropus eugenii 139
Macropus fuliginosus 144, 205
Macropus giganteus 106, 136, 144
Macropus irma 139
Macropus parma 140
Macropus parryi 112, 140
Macropus robustus 10, 143
Macropus rufogriseus 141
Macropus rufus 145
Macrotis lagotis 54, 61
Megaptera novaeangliae 185
Melomys burtoni 161
Myotis macropus 157
Myrmecobius fasciatus 48, 51
Neophoca cinerea 170, 174, 205
Notomys alexis 158, 162
Notoryctes typhlops 52–53
Nyctimene robinsoni 154
Onychogalea fraenata 134, 135
Onychogalea unguifera 135
Orcaella heinsohni 190
Orcinus orca 188
Ornithorhynchus anatinus 20, 23, 205
Oryctolagus cuniculus 195
Parantechinus apicalis 43
Perameles bougainville 59
Perameles gunnii 60
Perameles nasuta 60
Petauroides volans 92
Petaurus australis 86, 88
Petaurus breviceps 88

Petaurus gracilis 89
Petaurus norfolcensis 89
Petrogale assimilis 129
Petrogale brachyotis 129
Petrogale burbidgei 130
Petrogale concinna 130
Petrogale lateralis 131
Petrogale mareeba 131
Petrogale penicillata 126, 132
Petrogale persephone 133
Petrogale xanthopus 133
Petropseudes dahli 93
Phalanger intercastellanus 97
Phascogale tapoatafa 40, 45, 205
Phascolarctos cinereus 64, 69, 204
Physeter macrocephalus 187
Planigale maculata 46
Potorous longipes 115
Potorous tridactylus 115
Pseudantechinus bilarni 43
macdonnellensis 44
Pseudocheirus occidentalis 95
Pseudocheirus peregrinus 95
Pseudochirops archeri 76, 93
Pseudochirulus cinereus 94
Pseudochirulus herbertensis 90, 94
Pseudomys albocinereus 162
Pseudomys australis 163
Pseudomys calaby 163i
Pseudomys delicatulus 164

Pteropus alecto 152, 204
Pteropus conspicillatus 148, 152
Pteropus poliocephalus 153
Pteropus scapulatus 153
Rattus fuscipes 164
Rattus rattus 195
Rattus tunneyi 165
Rhinonicteris aurantius 156
Sarcophilus harrisii 36, 39
Setonix brachyurus 122
Sminthopsis crassicaudata 47
Sminthopsis virginiae 47
Sousa chinensis 190
Spilocuscus maculatus 98
Stenella coeruleoalba 191
Stenella longirostris 191
Sus scrofa 197

Syconycteris australia 154
Tachyglossus aculeatus 24, 27, 205
Taphozous georgianus 156
Tarsipes rostratus 100
Thylogale billardierii 120
Thylogale stigmatica 121
Thylogale thetis 120, 121
Trichosurus caninus 98, 204
Trichosurus vulpecula 96, 99
Tursiops truncatus 178, 189, 204
Vombatus ursinus 70, 74, 205
Vulpes vulpes 194
Wallabia bicolor 123
Wyulda squamicaudata 99
Zyzomys argurus 165

Abbreviations and Symbols

♂	male	**T**	length from base to tip of tail	
♀	female			
l	litre/s	**HBT**	length from tip of snout to end of tail	
t	tonne			
kg	kilogram/s	**CP**	Conservation Park	
g	gram/s	**NP**	National Park	
mg	milligram/s	**ACT**	Australian Capital Territory	
km	kilometre/s			
m	metre/s	**NT**	Northern Territory	
cm	centimetre/s	**NSW**	New South Wales	
mm	millimetre/s	**Qld**	Queensland	
kHz	kilohertz	**SA**	South Australia	
Hz	hertz	**Tas**	Tasmania	
°C	degrees Celsius	**Vic**	Victoria	
HB	length from tip of snout to base of tail	**WA**	Western Australia	

ACKNOWLEDGEMENTS

While the majority of the photographs in this book were taken in the wild, it was necessary to photograph rare or very shy species in several of Australia's zoos and fauna parks. A special thanks to the staff and management of Healesville Sanctuary, Victoria; Territory Wildlife Park, Northern Territory; Warrawong Earth Sanctuary, South Australia; Monarto Zoo, South Australia; Currumbin Wildlife Sanctuary, Queensland.

Text: Cath Jones

Thanks for their expertise and additional text to Steve Parish, the late Pat Slater, Dr Tom Grant and Dr Ian Gynther.

Photography and photographic design: Steve Parish

Additional photography as credited. Thanks to Ian Morris for reading the manuscript and supplying many of his photographs.

Publisher: Donald Greig

Editorial: Kate Lovett, Wynne Webber, Britt Winter and Karin Cox (SPP)

Cover design: Cristina Pecetta (SPP)

Design and finished art: Leanne Staff and Leanne Nobilio

Illustrations: Stephen Lee

Production: Tiffany Johnson

Left: Eastern Grey Kangaroo; Front cover: Squirrel Glider, Red Kangaroo (inset), Tasmanian Devil (inset), Short-beaked Echidna (inset); Back cover: Koala; Spinifex Hopping-mouse; Page 1: Green Possum; Pages 2–3: Sugar Glider (© Ian Morris); Page 4: Australian Sea-lion

© copyright Steve Parish Publishing Pty Ltd
PO Box 1058, Archerfield, Queensland 4108 Australia

ISBN 174021743 8

10 9 8 7 6 5 4 3 2 1

Parish, Steve, 1945- .
Guide to Australian mammals.

Includes index.
ISBN 1 74021 743 8.

1. Mammals - Australia. 2. Marsupials - Australia. 3. Monotremes - Australia. 4. Wildlife watching - Australia. I. Jones, Cath, 1953- . II. Title.

591.994

Printed in China by PrintPlus Ltd

Prepress by Colour Chiefs Digital Imaging, Australia

Produced in Australia at the Steve Parish Publishing Studio

online

FOR PRODUCTS
www.steveparish.com.au

FOR LIMITED EDITION PRINTS
www.steveparishexhibits.com.au

FOR PHOTOGRAPHY EZINE
www.photographaustralia.com.au